POCKET
TOKYO

Selena Takigawa Hoy, Cherise Fong,
Todd Fong, Rob Goss, Kim Kahan,
Louise George Kittaka, Manami Okazaki

Contents

Top: Kimono, Sensō-ji (p162)
Bottom: Sensō-ji, Asakusa (p159)

★ Top Experiences

★ Worth a Trip

The Journey Begins Here

Tokyo is never boring. I've lived here over half my life, and there are still so many corners that I haven't seen yet. I believe you could spend your whole life exploring this city and never truly see everything. Whether your scene is dining, music, art, architecture or a niche hobby unknown to the mainstream but with hundreds or thousands of devotees, Tokyo has you covered. The major sights are as impressive as advertised, but the true magic of Tokyo is wandering, finding serendipity in alleys, in a tiny standing bar, at a retro bathhouse or in a secret garden. Give yourself permission to get lost.
- *Selena Takigawa Hoy*

Selena Takigawa Hoy
@selenahoy

Selena is the Lonely Planet Destination Editor for Northeast Asia. She lives in Tokyo.

Todd Fong
@toddfong

Todd covered Marunouchi & Nihombashi and Ginza & Tsukiji, and walked between all of them repetitively.

Kim Kahan
kimjakahan.xyz

Kim writes about travel and culture all around Japan. She updated the Roppongi & Around chapter.

Louise George Kittaka

@louisegeorgekittaka

Originally from New Zealand, Louise is a Tokyo-based writer who chases waterfalls and sweet treats with equal enthusiasm, always willing to take the scenic (and tastier) route. She updated the Shinjuku & West Tokyo and Ghibli Museum chapters.

Tokyo Tower (p78)

Cherise Fong

@ishaam501

Cherise is a solo bicycle traveller who writes about travel, film, ecology and other art-science adventures. She updated the Shibuya & Ebisu chapter.

Rob Goss

@robgosswriter

Rob is a multi-award-winning writer from Dartmoor in the UK but has called the east side of Tokyo home for some 20 years. He updated the Harajuku & Aoyama and Ueno & Yanesen chapters.

Manami Okazaki

maki23.com

Manami is a journalist and curator. She has written 15 books on Japanese culture. She updated the Akihabara, Kōrakuen & Kagurazaka and Asakusa & Sumida River chapters.

Dining Experiences

Tokyo has a superlative dining scene that includes top-class sushi restaurants, oil-spattered noodle joints and everything in between. Tokyoites love dining out; join them and delight in the sheer variety of tastes and experiences the city has to offer.

Start the day with breakfast at **Tsukiji Outer Market**, a historic open-air market with food stalls and restaurants specialising in *kaisen-don* (raw fish on rice). (pictured left; p64)

Have dinner and drinks at an **izakaya** – Japan's version of a pub – where food and booze go hand-in-hand while the day's stresses dissolve into boisterous banter. (p126)

Descend to the lower levels of department stores and malls to find **depachika**, gourmet food halls filled with desserts, deli counters and gorgeously packaged gift items. (p63)

Go for *yakitori* (charcoal grilled skewers) and retro vibes at one of the small wooden counter restaurants at **Omoide-yokochō**, which means 'Memory Lane'. (p125)

Get a taste for *wagashi*, traditional Japanese sweets, at **Toraya**, a storied confectioner with an in-shop teahouse in Akasaka. (pictured right; p78)

Right: Omoide-yokochō (p125)

PLAN YOUR TRIP

Outdoor Experiences

Tokyo may be known for its concrete and neon streetscapes, but it is also surprisingly green. Take some time for the city's historic gardens – many centuries old – and public parks, all designed to be enjoyed year-round.

Soak up the atmosphere at **Meiji-jingū**, a Shintō shrine ensconced in a rare urban forest, with trees from all over Japan. (pictured left; p103)

Stroll along the **Meguro River** at Naka-Meguro, where it narrows to a canal – framed by cherry trees and flanked with stylish boutiques. (p97)

Sip green matcha alfresco while admiring the views at beautiful bayside garden, and former shogunate summer villa, **Hama-rikyū Onshi-teien**. (p59)

Hop on a **river cruise** in Nihombashi that takes you through the city's historic – and often overlooked – waterways. (p48)

Stretch out on the manicured, grassy lawns, have a picnic or peep at the spectacular orchids in the hothouse at urban retreat **Shinjuku-gyoen**. (pictured right; p120)

Paddle in the Imperial Palace moat at **Chidori-ga-fuchi** – especially a treat during cherry blossom season. (p49)

Right: Cherry blossoms, Chidori-ga-fuchi (p49)

PLAN YOUR TRIP

Shopping Experiences

Tokyo is a world-class shopping destination, with grand old department stores, trendsetting boutiques and a vibrant street-fashion scene. The city also has a strong artisanal tradition and a passion for *monozukuri* ('the art of making things').

Weave through the narrow lanes of **Ura-Hara** – the nickname for Harajuku's back streets – in search of novel looks and one-of-a-kind souvenirs. (p111)

Shop (or window-shop) your way through the designer fashions on display at the grand department stores and high-end malls in **Ginza**, Tokyo's classiest neighbourhood. (pictured left; p60)

Hunt for treasure among the secondhand and vintage stores of

Shimo-Kitazawa, a low-rise residential neighbourhood and popular bohemian haunt near Shibuya. (pictured right; p96)

Check out luxury styles – and visit the relocated teamLab Borderless – at **Azabudai Hills**, an upscale mega mall in the Roppongi area. (p72)

Take a detour to **Kuramae**, a district near Asakusa where many artisans have set up ateliers and shops, and the best place to find handmade, one-of-a-kind items. (p168)

After Dark Experiences

Tokyo is a work-hard, play-hard city, and you'll find bars full most any day of the week. But you don't have to drink to enjoy Tokyo after dark: most observatories are open late for spectacular nightscapes.

Score open-air views over Tokyo at night – when the city lights stretch as far as the eye can see – from landmark **Shibuya Sky**. (p87)

Clink glasses with local creatives and fellow travellers at **Golden Gai**, a bohemian hot spot in Shinjuku. (p122)

Go bar-hopping through **Ebisu**, the home of Yebisu beer. (p88)

See **Tokyo Tower** – a beloved symbol of the city – all lit up at night. (p78)

Have a big night out in **Dōgenzaka**, Shibuya's all-night party district. (p94)

Get your groove on in **Shinjuku Nichōme**, Tokyo's 'gaybourhood', home to hundreds of small bars and clubs. (p127)

View from Shibuya Sky (p87)

THE BEST
Art & Design Experiences

Tokyo has established itself as a top-tier destination for contemporary art and architecture, especially digital art. It's a reputation that only grows stronger as new museums open and ever more innovative structures go up.

Immerse yourself in the fluid, ever-changing world of the interactive responsive art museum **teamLab Borderless**, one of Tokyo's most popular attractions. (p72)

Get schooled in Japanese art history at the **Tokyo National Museum**, the finest collection of Japanese art and cultural artefacts in the world. (p149)

Catch the latest blockbuster exhibition at the **Mori Art Museum**, a sky-high space for contemporary art at Roppongi Hills. (pictured left; p73)

Be awed by the contemporary architecture, the work of Japan's leading architects, along leafy boulevard **Omotesandō**. (p108)

Visit the **Nezu Museum**, where classical works of Japanese, Korean and Chinese art are displayed in a striking contemporary building. (pictured right; p108)

Ponder the role of design in everyday life at **21_21 Design Sight**, a unique cultural institution at Tokyo Midtown. (p76)

Right: teamLab Borderless: MORI Building DIGITAL ART MUSEUM (p72)

PLAN YOUR TRIP

THE BEST

Traditional Culture Experiences

You don't need to take the bullet train to Kyoto to experience traditional Japanese culture. Get a taste for it at Tokyo's many Shintō shrines and Buddhist temples, and via classic spectacles such as kabuki, sumo and *matsuri* (traditional festivals).

Soak up the atmosphere (and the incense) at **Sensō-ji**, Tokyo oldest temple – more than 1000 years older than the city itself. (p162)

Swoon at the cherry blossoms at **Shinjuku-gyoen**, a classic Tokyo destination for *hanami* (cherry-blossom-viewing parties). (p120)

See kabuki – Japan's signature performing art – at **Kabuki-za**, Tokyo's dedicated kabuki theatre, which

celebrated its centennial in 2024. (pictured left; p57)

Catch the salt-slinging, belly-slapping ritual of sumo at one of the three annual tournaments held at **Ryōgoku Kokugikan**. (pictured right; p168)

Step back in time at one of many **traditional festivals**, which feature parades, chanting, costumes and more, carried out just as they have been for centuries. (p169)

Right: Sanja Matsuri (p169), Asakusa

PLAN YOUR TRIP

Akihabara (p137)

THE BEST

Pop Culture Experiences

From Godzilla to Studio Ghibli, Hello Kitty to Pokémon, Japanese pop culture has captivated the world for generations. Tokyo is where you get to see – and experience – the scenes from your screens in 3D.

You've seen it in films, video games and social media, now see Tokyo's iconic intersection **Shibuya Scramble Crossing** in real life. (p85)

Explore **Akihabara**, the centre of Tokyo's *otaku* (geek) subculture, home to neon-bright electronics stores, cosplay cafes and multi-storey anime and manga shops. (p137)

Experience the magical world of master animator, and recent Academy Award–winner, Hayao Miyazaki at the **Ghibli Museum, Mitaka**. (p132)

Spot style trends past and present along Harajuku's signature shopping street, **Takeshita-dōri**. (p109)

Head to **Nakano Broadway**, a fascinating vintage shopping centre full of subculture shops, including the original Mandarake Complex. (p121)

Indulge your inner child at **Kiddy Land**, Tokyo's most famous toy store, full of all your character faves – from Hello Kitty to Super Mario. (p107)

THE BEST

Historic Tokyo Experiences

Before Tokyo became Tokyo, it was Edo, the shogun's capital. Traces of this older city remain, as do relics and reminders from other eras of the city's fascinating 400-year history.

Visit the **Imperial Palace**, where Edo-jō – the shogun's castle – once stood, and where parts of it, including foundation walls, watchtowers and moats, remain. (pictured left; p42)

Cross **Nihonbashi**, Tokyo's most famous bridge, guarded by bronze lions and winged *kirin* (mythical dragon-like creatures), and the official city centre. (p46)

Absorb the sights, sounds and smells of **Ameya-yokochō**, an old-fashioned outdoor market that dates to the mid-20th century. (pictured right; p151)

Explore **Yanaka**, the rare Tokyo neighbourhood where traditional wooden buildings, from the turn of the last century, predominate. (p152)

Learn about life in old Edo at the **Edo-Tokyo Museum**, Tokyo's excellent local history museum, due to re-open in 2026 after extensive renovations. (p169)

Stroll the centuries-old cobblestone streets of **Azabu-jūban**, a village-like district just a stone's throw from Roppongi. (p76)

Yoyogi-kōen (p108)

THE BEST

Local Experiences

Get to know Tokyo from a local perspective by heading to one their favourite haunts or indulging in a popular leisure activity – such as trawling the farmers market or seeing a baseball game.

Hit the weekend **Farmers Market @ UNU** in Aoyama for food trucks, gourmet goods, special events and all-round good vibes. (p110)

Cheer on the Yomiuri Giants, one of Tokyo's two baseball teams – and the one that's won the most championships – at **Tokyo Dome**, aka the Big Egg. (p139)

Browse the secondhand bookshops in **Jimbōchō**, a popular destination for generations of students, and also popular for its cafes and curry shops. (p142)

Visit a *sentō* (bathhouse), such as Aoyama's **Shimizu-yu**, for a good, long soak – perfect after a day of sightseeing or for transitioning from day to evening. (p111)

Join Tokyoites of all stripes – including a group of retro greasers dancing around a boom box – at Harajuku's beloved public park, **Yoyogi-kōen**. (p108)

Best for Kids

Let older children take the lead at awe-inspiring **teamLab Borderless**, and don't miss Sketch Factory – a highlight for kids. (p72)

Introduce kids to your favourite games at the arcades in **Akihabara**, many of which have vintage machines for playing the likes of Mario Kart and Street Fighter. (p137)

Let little ones run off steam on the large, grassy expanse that is **Yoyogi-kōen**, a public park popular with local families. (p108)

Take your tweens and teens to **Takeshita-dōri**, where they can sample the latest street food and pick out a trendy item or two to impress friends back home. (p109)

Plan a side trip to the **Ghibli Museum, Mitaka**, a museum for all ages that rewards exploration (and has a special treat for under-12s). (p132)

Best for Free

Explore the grounds of **Sensō-ji**, which is one of Tokyo's top attractions and, like most temples and shrines in the city, totally free to visit. (p162)

Skip the admission fees at the city's other observatories and get your views for nothing – day or night – atop the **Tokyo Metropolitan Government Building** in Shinjuku. (p126)

Take the pulse of the city's art scene at **Complex 665**, a collection of contemporary galleries down the street from the Mori Art Museum. (p76)

Bask in the frenetic energy of **Shibuya Scramble Crossing**, the unintentional tourist attraction that's become a symbol of the city. (p85)

Visit the **East Garden** at the Imperial Palace – free, unlike most gardens – where highlights include the ruins of an old castle *donjon* (main keep). (p42)

Perfect Days

It would take a lifetime to do Tokyo justice, but you can accomplish a surprising amount in a short time if you plan accordingly. That's where these itineraries come in.

Golden Gai (p122)

DAY ONE

With Only One Day

MORNING

Start with a visit to **Meiji-jingū** (pictured above; p103), one of Tokyo's top attractions, best visited early in the day. From here you can explore famous fashion district **Harajuku** (p106), also home to many excellent cafes and lunch spots.

AFTERNOON

Continue your tour of westside highlights in Shibuya, home to the iconic intersection, **Shibuya Scramble Crossing** (p85). Take in views of the neighbourhood from landmark **Shibuya Sky** (p87).

EVENING

Shinjuku – one of Tokyo's principle districts – is also Tokyo's largest nightlife areas. Visit retro dining and drinking alley **Omoide-yokochō** (p126) for *yakitori* (charcoal-grilled skewers) and **Golden Gai** (p122) for its maze of tiny, bohemian bars.

DAY TWO

A Weekend Trip

MORNING

Tsukiji Outer Market (pictured above; p64) is a top experience that rewards an early start; come to cobble together a fresh seafood breakfast from the many vendors. Then walk it off among the serene strolling paths at traditional garden **Hama-rikyū Onshi-teien** (p59).

AFTERNOON

Head to upscale **Ginza** (p60) for a spot of kabuki – Japan's signature performing art – at historic theatre **Kabuki-za** (p57). Elsewhere in Ginza, look for grand old department stores, dessert parlours and classic *kissaten* (vintage early 20th-century cafes; p63).

EVENING

Then make your way to nearby **Nihombashi** for historic restaurants (p51) and swanky hotel bars – a fine way to end the day.

DAY THREE

A Short Break

MORNING

See more of traditional Tokyo in east-side hub Ueno, home to sprawling **Ueno-kōen** (p152), where attractions include the Tokyo National Museum and historical shrines and temples, all linked by strolling paths.

AFTERNOON

From here, continue your stroll through **Yanaka** (p152), a charming neighbourhood known for its intact early 20th-century streetscapes (and sunning cats).

EVENING

As the sun begins to drop, head to **Asakusa** (p159) to see the grand old temple, **Sensō-ji** (p162), another top sight. It's jammed during the day but quieter by dusk (and illuminated in the evenings). Then consider dinner with a view at **Tokyo Skytree** (pictured above; p164) just over the river.

If You Have More Time

With more time, you can go beyond the main attractions and just hang out. Tokyo is full of fascinating neighbourhoods where sightseeing can take a back seat to unstructured exploration. If you're into Japanese pop culture – especially anime, manga and gaming – **Akihabara** (p137) is probably already on your list; even if you're not, it's worth checking out this famous neighbourhood, just to see what it's all about.

You can also head west of Shinjuku, to the neighbourhoods along the Chūō line, each of which have their own vibe. **Nakano** (p129) is a subculture hot spot with a charmingly chaotic retro shopping arcade; while laid-back **Kōenji** (p128) is a counter-culture hub that's ace for shopping. Both get a late start, so don't arrive before noon. The same goes for other bargain hot spot **Shimo-Kitazawa** (p96), and fashionable neighbourhoods **Daikanyama** and **Naka-Meguro** (p97); these three are within easy striking distance of Shibuya.

Akihabara (p137)

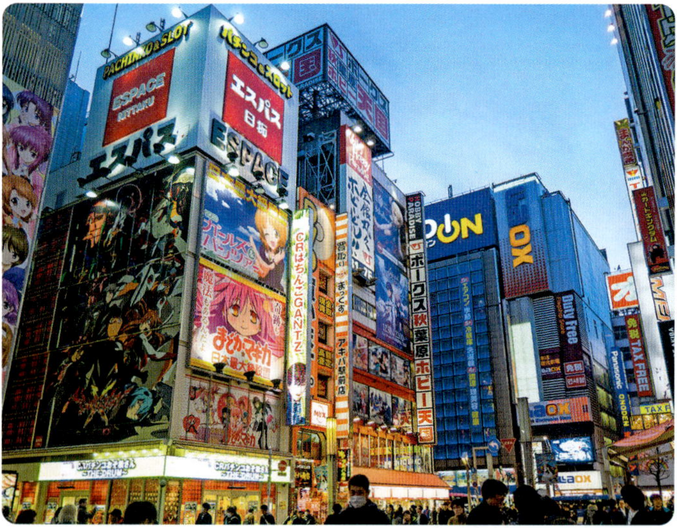

A City Day Trip

Take a worthwhile detour to the enchanting **Ghibli Museum, Mitaka** (p132). It was designed by master animator Hayao Miyazaki himself and is full of references to his beloved Studio Ghibli films. The museum is in Mitaka, one of Tokyo's western suburbs and a 20-minute train ride from Shinjuku. This is one attraction Hayao Miyazaki for which you'll need to plan ahead: advanced bookings are required and they do go fast. The museum is part of a larger park, **Inokashira-kōen** (pictured above; p133); it's one of Tokyo's best, and you can enjoy a stroll on your way there or back.

On a Rainy Day

Tokyo has plenty of museums perfect for soaking up rainy days. You can easily spend hours exploring the **Tokyo National Museum** (pictured above; p149), the world's largest collection of Japanese art. For something contemporary, check out what's on at the **Mori Art Museum** (p73); **teamLab Borderless** (p72) at Azabudai Hills is another option, though advanced booking is required.

Another option is to spend the day (or night) trying out the various baths and saunas at **Shimizu-yu** (p111), a public bathhouse right in the middle of the city. And don't forget about **karaoke** (p94), another weatherproof activity and classic Tokyo experience.

Get Prepared

BOOK AHEAD

Two months before
Scan the web for upcoming tours, exhibitions, festivals or events.

One month in advance
Book tickets for popular sights, such as teamLab Borderless and the Ghibli Museum, Mitaka, as well as tables at sought-after restaurants.

One week in advance
As your plans firm up, consider making reservations for other restaurants, especially for Friday and Saturday nights.

Manners Matter

As densely populated as Tokyo is, a high degree of consideration for others is required to keep the whole operation running as efficiently as it does.

Queueing is important, as is keeping a low profile in public settings; for example, it's best to refrain from talking loudly on the subway or bringing over-sized suitcases on the train during rush hour. Eating in public is also frowned upon, except in places where food vendors congregate, such as festivals and markets.

What to Pack

Dress for comfort with supportive shoes; you'll likely be walking a lot. Tokyoites are smart but usually practical dressers. Only the highest-end restaurants and bars have enforced dress codes, which usually just means no sleeveless shirts or sandals on men. Religious sights (Buddhist temples and Shintō shrines) have no dress codes. Keep in mind that you may be taking your shoes on and off so slip-on ones are handy.

Things to Know

Mondays Most museums close on Mondays (or on the following Tuesday if Monday is a national holiday).

Lunch Locals know to splurge at lunch when high-end restaurants often offer lower-priced menus (with the same great food).

Touts Steer clear of strangers trying to coax you into bars and clubs, lest you end up with a bill that's more than you bargained for.

Shoes off Some traditional restaurants and inns request you leave your shoes at the door. Shoes should never be worn on tatami mats.

Escalators Stand to the left.

TIPPING

Tipping is not customary in Japan, nor expected – except in the case of tour guides. Many bars and restaurants, however, do add service fees to the bill. This may come in the form of an *otoshi,* a per-person cover charge (around ¥300 to ¥1000) that includes an appetiser or snacks. High-end restaurants and bars (such as those at luxury hotels) tend to add a service fee of 10% to 15% to the bill instead.

DAILY BUDGET

Budget: Less than ¥15,000

- Dorm bed per person: **¥5000**
- Free sights such as temples and markets
- Bowl of noodles: **¥1200**
- Happy-hour drink: **¥800**
- 24-hour subway pass: **¥600**

Midrange: ¥15,000–30,000

- Double room at a business hotel: **¥20,000**
- Museum entry: **¥1000**
- Dinner for two with drinks at an *izakaya* (Japanese pub-eatery): **¥10,000**
- Fancy cocktail: **¥2000**

Top End: More than ¥30,000

- Double room in a four-star hotel: from **¥40,000**
- Cooking class: **¥10,000**
- Tasting course per person: **¥30,000**
- Taxi ride back to the hotel: **¥4000**

Currency
Japanese yen (¥)

Language
Japanese

Time zone
Japan Standard Time (GMT/UTC plus nine hours)

CASH

While credit cards are now widely accepted in Tokyo, you will still encounter small businesses where cash is king. Fortunately, the city's ubiquitous convenience stores have ATMs that usually work with overseas cards.

When to Go

Tokyo is year-round destination and there's no bad time to visit. Each season has its own highlights.

Spring is the most popular time of year to visit, followed by autumn. This is when the weather is the most pleasant, with warm, mostly sunny days and cool nights (though April can still be chilly).

June brings the rainy season, which can last through July; rain (and wind!) can also be an issue when typhoons roll through in September and October. August is hot and humid, which many visitors find uncomfortable. Winter, which sees the fewest visitors, is chilly but rarely freezing, with generally clear skies.

The Big Events

January **Hatsu-mōde**, the first shrine visit of the new year, starts just after midnight on 1 January. Meiji-jingū is Tokyo's most popular destination, drawing 3 million people over the first few days of the year.

April Late March or early April brings the **cherry blossoms** – for just a week or two – and Tokyoites toast them with spirited parties, called *hanami*, under the boughs in parks and along riverbanks city-wide.

May Tokyo's biggest *matsuri* (traditional festival) is Asakusa's **Sanja Matsuri** (p169), which sees rollicking parades of *mikoshi* (portable shrines) carried by men in short coats and *fundoshi* (the loincloths worn by sumo wrestlers) – and more than a million spectators.

July Summer is the season for fireworks and Tokyo's grandest display, the **Sumidagawa Fireworks Festival**, features 20,000 pyrotechnic wonders exploding over the city's principal waterway.

Tokyo Weather

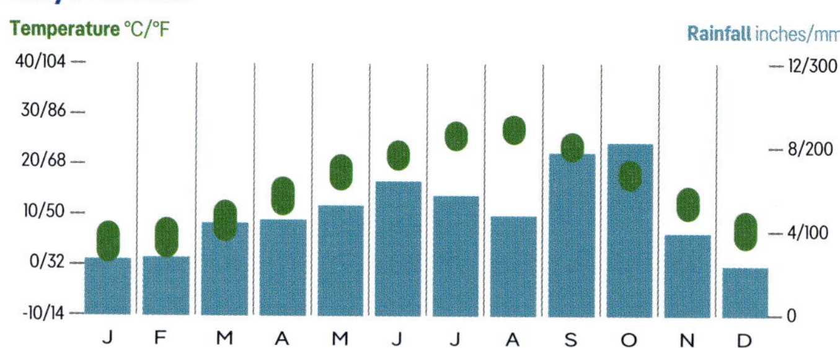

Kōenji Awa Odori

August Kōenji Awa Odori is Tokyo's biggest outdoor dance party – of the traditional kind. Over 10,000 participants, in kimonos and peaked straw hats, take to the streets to perform folk dances accompanied by musicians.

Arts & Pop Culture Events

March Anime Japan has events and exhibitions for industry insiders and fans alike, but it is most famous for attracting Japan's top cosplayers – and increasingly international ones, too.

July & November Design Festa, organised by the Harajuku gallery of the same name (p112), is an off-the-wall DIY art fair that features performances and thousands of exhibitors.

September Dazzling spectacles and larger-than-life installations take over Roppongi's streets and commercial complexes during **Roppongi Art Night** (p79), which goes on until the next day.

September At **Tokyo Game Show** you can preview the latest games, consoles and entertainment tech innovations. There are also fun events such as the Street Fighter pro tour.

ACCOMMODATION LOWDOWN

Occupancy is highest at weekends and during holiday periods, like Golden Week (late April to early May) and the week around New Year. Hostels and traditional inns often have fixed prices while everywhere else uses dynamic pricing – which can fluctuate wildly. Booking ahead is always recommended.

✈ Getting There

Narita Airport, in neighbouring Chiba Prefecture, is the main entry point, and where most budget flights arrive. Increasingly, international routes are flying to Haneda Airport, which is near Tokyo Bay and closer to the city centre.

From Narita Airport to the City Centre

By Train

Two rail lines run express services between Narita Airport and central Tokyo. The JR Narita Express (N'EX) has a direct service to Tokyo, Shinjuku and Yokohama; travel takes 60 to 90 minutes and tickets start at ¥3000.

The Keisei Skyliner travels to Nippori and Ueno in cast Tokyo in under an hour for about ¥2500. There are also slower, local trains for budget travellers. At any arrival station, catch onward travel via the JR Yamanote line, select subway lines or taxi.

At Narita Airport, the train stations are in the basements of terminals 1 and 2; coming from terminal 3, walk or take the free shuttle bus to terminal 2. Purchase tickets from kiosks (in person) or from the automated machines at the station.

By Bus

Coaches travel from all terminals at Narita Airport to destinations around central Tokyo. The journey takes about 1½ hours, depending on traffic. Reserved-seat limousine buses cost around ¥3000; purchase at the airport or online in advance. There are also cheaper, pay-when-you-board coaches that cost around ¥1000, but have limited destinations and stricter luggage restrictions.

By Taxi

Expect to pay around ¥25,000 to ¥30,000 for a fixed-fare taxi to central Tokyo (depending on your destination). Pick up taxis from the kerb.

From Haneda Airport

All overseas flights to Haneda arrive at the international terminal, from where you can take the Keikyū Airport Express to Shinagawa (*¥330, 12 minutes*) or the Tokyo Monorail to Hamamatsuchō (*¥520, 20 minutes*). Both stations are stops on the JR Yamanote line for easy onward connections.

Taxis from Haneda are more reasonable, around ¥7000 to ¥10,000, depending on where you're going. There are coaches too, but these really only make sense if you're arriving after the trains stop running around midnight. If you're taking a late-night taxi, there's a 20% surcharge between 10pm and 5am (same for Narita). Credit cards are accepted.

Getting Around

Tokyo's public transport system is the envy of cities around the world: it's clean, reliable, inexpensive and (generally) safe. The rail network, which is multilingual and easy to navigate, can take you almost anywhere you want to go. Taxis, while plentiful, are expensive in comparison. For the intrepid, cycling is an option.

Train & Metro

Tokyo's rail network, which includes train and metro, runs from approximately 5am to midnight. The line you'll probably use the most is the elevated JR Yamanote, which traces a loop around the city centre, stopping at major hubs such as Shinjuku, Shibuya, Shinagawa, Akihabara and Ueno. The Chūō line runs east to west through the centre, connecting Shinjuku with Tokyo Station. Meanwhile, a myriad of private commuter lines depart in every direction for the suburbs.

Taxis & Rideshares

Taxis are your only all-night transport option. Train stations and major hotels have designated taxi stands; otherwise you can hail a cab from the street by standing on the curb and holding out your arm. A sign with 空車 means the taxi is free; otherwise it's reserved.

Tokyo strictly regulates ride-sharing apps. You can only use them to summon licensed taxis (at regular prices) and fancier, more expensive town cars.

FROM LEFT: PORNPRASIT PANADA/SHUTTERSTOCK, KENSOFTTH/SHUTTERSTOCK

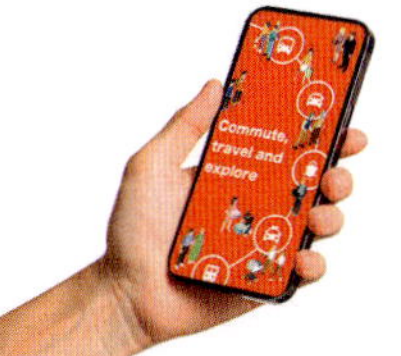

ESSENTIAL APP

Japan Transit Planner – the English version of a popular Japanese navigation app – generates public transport routes and has helpful maps.

Walking

Walking is a great way to get around. In the city centre the distance between two metro stations is rarely more than 10 minutes – you'll save a little yen and see a more local side of the city. Just note that outside major hubs pavements are scarce and Tokyo can be rather hilly.

Cycling

Tokyo has a few different bike-sharing schemes, though they require setting up an account in advance. Docomo Cycle has the largest network and basic instructions online in English. These (and most rental cycles in Tokyo) are electric-assist bikes – an experience if you've never ridden one before. Some hostels and inns also have (regular) bikes to lend.

Cycling in Tokyo can be a little intense with the traffic. You'll also need to be careful to park in designated spots so that your bike doesn't get confiscated.

Bus

Tokyo has an extensive bus network, though it's rarely more convenient than the subway and is harder to navigate.

Public Transport Essentials

Tap Cards

While you can still buy paper tickets, it's much easier to use a prepaid tap card. There are two kinds, Suica (sold at JR stations) and Pasmo (sold at metro and commuter-line stations). It doesn't matter which one you get; both work on all train, subway and bus routes in Tokyo (and many routes outside of Tokyo, too). They can also be used to pay for taxis, convenience-store purchases and many vending machines.

Purchase and top-up tap cards at the automatic ticket machines found in train and subway stations. There's a ¥500 deposit required, which you can get back (along with any remaining charge) by returning the card to a corresponding station counter (at a JR station for Suica, for example). At either airport, look out for the discount 'Welcome Suica' exclusively for foreign tourists, which doesn't require a deposit (and is meant as a keepsake).

Transferring

Tokyo's rail network is managed by multiple operators, which can make transferring confusing. There's JR, two metro operators (Tokyo Metro and Toei), plus the commuter rail companies. Transferring between lines run by the same operator is straightforward. Transfer between operators and you'll have to tap out and tap in again at different gates, and possibly walk a fair bit; you're also stuck paying both operators.

24-Hour Travel Passes

Depending on how much you plan to do in a day (and the routes you'll take), 24-hour tickets can be a good deal. Be sure to read the fine print, however: the cheapest option, which costs ¥800, is only good on Tokyo Metro lines. Tickets can be purchased from the automated ticket machines, or from kiosks at select stations.

FINDING THE RIGHT EXIT

Train stations often have multiple exits and it's worth taking time to get your bearings and pick the right one. Maps within the stations are a big help.

TICKETS

Single ride ticket fares are calculated by distance travelled.

Ticket type	Good for	Cost
Single ride within Tokyo	One-way travel on JR, Tokyo Metro or Toei lines	¥150-330
Tokyo Metro 24-hour ticket	Unlimited rides on Tokyo Metro lines	¥800
Tokyo Combination 24-hour ticket	Unlimited rides on Tokyo Metro and Toei subway lines, JR lines in Tokyo	¥1600

🎁 A Few Surprises

Tokyo is full of big-ticket attractions, but a lot of the city's charm lies in the details. Don't forget to look up, down – and underground.

Station Cities

The Tokyo metropolitan area is one of the world's largest built spaces, and that's only taking into account what's above ground. There are whole parallel cities underneath some of the city's largest train stations, including **Shinjuku Station** (p129)– the world's busiest, in terms of daily passenger rate – and Tokyo Station, the city's central station and terminus for the bullet-train network. Explore these underground passages and you'll find all kinds of places to eat, drink and shop. In the aptly named Tokyo Station City, for example, you can visit **Tokyo Ramen Street** (p41) for a hot meal or **Tokyo Character Street** (p41) for souvenir shopping.

Godzilla on the Loose

Ever since Godzilla, called Gojira in Japanese, first rose from the sea in 1954, the monster has been a worldwide object of fascination. Godzilla has destroyed Tokyo multiple times on film and now threatens to do so from multiple locations around the city. The biggest tourist attraction is the huge **Godzilla Head** (p125) statue in Shinjuku's Kabukichō, poised to take a bite out of the Toho Building. There's also a statue of **Shin-Godzilla** by the Toho Cinema in Hibiya (Toho is the film company that produces the Godzilla franchise; p73). Meanwhile, diehard fans will know Shinagawa as the site of Godzilla's first appearance, and there are a few Easter eggs in the area. On weekends, catch the newest addition: Godzilla projected in a dazzling light show on the **Tokyo Metropolitan Government Building** (p124) as part of the city's Tokyo Night & Light projection mapping project.

Shopping Street Signs

As visitors to Tokyo are quick to learn, few streets actually have names. Those that do are usually either major thoroughfares or pedestrianised market streets, called *shōtengai*. These are often marked by gates – not dissimilar to *torii* (shrine gates), but with colourful signs announcing the name of the street. Most of these date to the mid-20th century and are a classic example of Tokyo's vernacular architecture (not to mention great for photos). Two you're likely to encounter are at the entrances to Harajuku's **Takeshita-dōri** (p109), where youth fashion and sweet treats reign, and Ueno's **Ameya-yokochō** (p151), home to cheap sneakers and cheerful sidewalk drinking joints. Further afield, ramble **Kōenji Pal Shopping Street** (p128) and **Look Street** (p128) for thrift scores and funky cafes in Kōenji, and **Nakano Broadway** (p121) for toys and manga. Stroll **Yanaka Ginza** (p153) near Ueno for secondhand kimonos and traditional street snacks.

Designer Loos

You may have seen them on social media – or featured in the latest Wim Wenders film *Perfect Days* (2023): Tokyo's designer loos are the latest hot tourist attraction. Launched in 2020, the Tokyo Toilet Project saw 20 public toilet facilities re-imagined by some of Japan's top architects and designers. They are all located within Shibuya ward, which includes Shibuya proper as well as Harajuku and Ebisu. The most popular one can be found near **Yoyogi-kōen** (p108), near Yoyogi-kōen metro station. Designed by Shigeru Ban, the facility appears transparent – until you

Godzilla Head (p125), Shinjuku

Ginkgo Avenue (p112), Aoyama

enter and lock the door, after which it becomes opaque. See our Ebisu Tokyo Toilet walking tour on p92.

Vintage Cafes

Tokyo has scores of trendy third-wave cafes and micro-roasters outdoing themselves to impress, but the city's coffee culture runs much deeper than that. The first generation of coffee shops, called *kissaten*, opened in the early decades of the 20th century, introducing coffee culture to a country new to the caffeinated buzz of coffee beans. A few of these vintage cafes still exist, atmospheric with low tables and chairs or banquettes, plus plenty of dark wood. In addition to retro decor, you'll often find dedicated (often elderly) staff, assiduously preparing pour-over brews or presiding over bubbling siphon percolators. Don't expect to see espresso machines or non-dairy milks here; thick toasts and diminutive slices of cake are the usual accompaniments. Ginza has several, including Tokyo's oldest, **Cafe Paulista** (p63), and the gentle **Cafe de l'Ambre** (p66); in

Shibuya, **Lion** (p95) serves coffee and classical music. In Ueno, try **Kayaba Coffee** (p157), set in an old wooden house with tatami-mat seating, or house-roasted coffee beans at **Café Lapin** (p157). Secondhand bookstore district **Jimbōchō** is also a great retro cafe destination (p142).

Beyond Cherry Blossoms

While the cherry blossoms get all the attention, they're hardly the only natural attractions Tokyo has to offer. A month earlier, bright pink plum blossoms appear on boughs in parks such as **Yoyogi-kōen** (p108). Later in spring, head to **Nezu-jinja** (p154) for spectacular azaleas or **Meiji-jingū Gyoen** (p104) for irises in myriad hues. Even the rainy season has its charms, in the form of glorious hydrangeas that pop up around town.

In late November and early December, the city's trees undergo magnificent seasonal transformations during *kōyō* (autumn foliage season); this is another excuse for garden visits. **Koishikawa Kōrakuen** (p138) and **Hama-rikyū Onshi-teien** (p59) are especially good for flaming red and orange maples, and the garden at the **Nezu Museum** (p108) in Aoyama is picture-perfect with its maples, ponds and stone lanterns. Meanwhile, Tokyo's official tree,

the ginkgo, turns an electrifying golden-yellow; see them in all their glory along the aptly named **Ginkgo Avenue** (p112). And in the winter, Tokyoites love illuminations, decorating the bare branches of tree-lined streets with millions of fairy lights, such as **Keiyaki-zaka** (p75) in Roppongi; the view frames the warming glow of **Tokyo Tower** (p78) in the near distance.

OFFBEAT TOKYO
- Check out the modern-day cabinet of curiosities that is **Intermediatheque** (p49), one of Tokyo's more eccentric attractions (and free to boot!).
- Visit Akihabara's signature shrine, **Kanda Myōjin** (p142), which features *omamori* (amulets) to protect your electronic devices and *ema* (votive tablets) decorated with anime figures.
- Enter a flower shop to discover a magical teahouse in the back at **Aoyama Flower Market's Green House** (p111).
- Shop for artisanal goods at **2k540 Aki-Oka Artisan** (p145), located under the elevated JR Yamanote line tracks between Akihabara and Okachimachi.
- Visit the **Art Aquarium Museum** (p64) where goldfish take centre stage.

Explore Tokyo

Worth a Trip

Tokyo's Walking Tours

Shibuya Scramble Crossing (p85)
ANEK.SOOWANNAPHOOM/SHUTTERSTOCK

See p51
for eating,
drinking and
shopping
listings

Explore
Marunouchi & Nihombashi

Researched by Todd Fong

Marunouchi (丸ノ内) sprang to life in the late 19th century, featuring the grand Tokyo Station and European-inspired architecture that announced Japan's emergence onto the world's stage after nearly three centuries of seclusion. Down a wide boulevard from the station are the moat-surrounded grounds of the Imperial Palace, once home to Edo Castle, but now a peaceful patch of greenery in the city centre with a lovely public garden.

On the opposite side of the station, a historic bridge marks Nihombashi (日本橋), Tokyo's first commercial district where all Japanese roads once led. Today, a handful of businesses established here nearly four centuries ago still remain, a tribute to Nihombashi's resilience.

Getting Around

 Train
Tokyo Station is served by many JR train lines including the Yamanote line that circles the central city. It is also the terminal for many shinkansen lines.

 Metro
There are many metro stations in the Marunouchi and Nihombashi area, served by the Ginza, Marunouchi, Hibiya, Tōzai, Chiyoda, Hanzōmon and Mita lines. Underground is a maze of passageways with shops and restaurants connecting the stations.

 Walk
A stroll from the Imperial Palace to Nihombashi is pleasant and can be done in about 20 minutes.

Tokyo Station (p41)
IAN.CUIYI/GETTY IMAGES

★

THE BEST

SEASONAL ACTIVITY
Marunouchi Winter Illuminations (p49)

FREE MUSEUM
Intermediatheque (p49)

BAR WITH A VIEW
Virtù (p52)

OUTDOOR ACTIVITY
Boating in the Chidori-ga-fuchi (p49) moat

UNIQUE SHOPPING CENTRE
KITTE (p49)

Hario Lampwork Factory

Ozu Washi

Shuto Expwy No 1

Shin-nihombashi

Chūō-dōri

Cohana

Mitsukoshimae

Nihonbashi Cruise

Riverboat Mizuha

Nihonbashi

Haibara

Mitsui Memorial Museum

Bank of Japan Currency Museum

Shuto Expwy No 5

NIHOMBASHI

Shuto Expwy No 1

KYŌBASHI

CHŪŌ-KU

Kayabachō

Kyōbashi

Showa-dōri

Yaesu-dōri

Chūō-dōri

Sakura-dōri

YAESU

Sotobori-dōri

Tokyo Station Gallery

Tokyo Station

Tokyo Character Street

Tokyo Ramen Street

KITTE

JR East Travel Service Center

Tokyo Station

Marunouchi Ekimae Square

Intermediatheque

JNTO Tourist Information Center

YŪRAKUCHŌ

Yūrakuchō

Kajibashi-dōri

ŌTEMACHI

Ōtemachi

Eitai-dōri

Naka-dōri

Uchibori-dōri

MARUNOUCHI

Nijūbashimae

Hibiya-dōri

Kōkyo-gaien Plaza

Sakuradamon

Harumi-dōri

CHIYODA-KU

Chidori-ga-fuchi

Imperial Palace East Garden

Sannomaru Shōzōkan

Imperial Palace

Fushimi-yagura

Nijū-bashi

For more see

Top Experiences p41
Experiences p48
Eating p51
Drinking p52
Shopping p53

400 m

0.2 miles

Tokyo Station

More than just a transit hub, Tokyo Station is an architectural masterpiece with two distinct faces, an extensive shopping mall, and a smorgasbord of bars and restaurants representing every genre all rolled into one.

MAP: P40 **D3**

Photograph Her Best Side

WWII air raids significantly damaged Tokyo Station; a full restoration of the building was completed in 2012, almost a century after it was first built. The western Marunouchi face of the station is an iconic Tokyo view and particularly beautiful at night. Shoot it head on from **Marunouchi Ekimae Square** or get a side profile from the rooftop of the **KITTE** (p49) shopping centre.

Tokyo Station Gallery

Visit the **Tokyo Station Gallery** (*ejrcf.or.jp/ gallery/english/; prices vary*) to get a closer look at the dome's upper floors. Around five exhibitions show here every year, though English signage may be sparse. Between areas of the gallery, you'll see exposed brick and other elements used in the original station construction.

The Streets of Tokyo Station

For character merchandise in one convenient location, **Tokyo Character Street** in the station underground complex has you covered. While exclusive items are few, kids and collectors can tick off many items from their shopping lists here. **Tokyo Ramen Street**, another favourite, consists of 10 of the city's best ramen shops, representing a variety of types from classic soy sauce to umami-packed sardine broth. There's almost always a queue here, so plan accordingly.

PLANNING TIP
If you're planning a Tokyo Station shopping and dining experience, avoid the weekends and shoot for a weekday afternoon when the station is the least crowded.

Scan this QR code for comprehensive information about Tokyo Station.

EXPLORE

MARUNOUCHI & NIHOMBASHI

Imperial Palace

When the military rule of the shogunate ended in the mid 19th century, the former Edo Castle grounds became the home of Japan's Imperial Family. The East Garden of the palace is open to the public, but much of the palace grounds can only be seen on a guided tour *(free)*.

MAP: P40 **A3**

PLANNING TIP
Book your spot on the tour online early – up to a month in advance. On the tour, you'll be on your feet for up to 1½ hours.

Scan this QR code for the online application for the Imperial Palace tour.

The Original Edo Castle

Edo-jō (Edo Castle) was originally built and occupied by the Tokugawa shogunate on the land the Imperial Palace now sits on. In 1868, the castle became the official residence of the Imperial Family when the shogunate was overthrown and Tokyo became the capital. Structures that remain from the Edo period are scarce, however – just two watchtowers, the stone walls and the gates.

Palace Buildings

The palace compound is relatively new, having been rebuilt in the 1960s following WWII air raids that destroyed much of it. One of the buildings you'll see on the tour is Kyūden – an understated, modern building where the throne room is located. You'll also see **Fushimi-yagura**, a watchtower from the Edo period, along with several modern statehouses. Another notable structure here is **Nijū-bashi**, an ornate steel bridge that serves as the official entrance to the palace.

The Tour

While being allowed into certain areas of the palace compound, visitors are unable to enter the buildings. It's still worth going on the tour to

©TOOYKRUB/SHUTTERSTOCK

learn more about the castle's past and present from knowledgeable guides, and the tour is free to boot – and available in multiple languages (English, French, Spanish, Chinese and Korean). Two tours are held each day from Tuesdays to Saturdays, except in summer from 1 July to 30 September, when only the morning tour is offered. No tours are offered on national holidays. If you missed your opportunity to book, you can try to arrive early and register on the spot, but space is not guaranteed. If all else fails, the Imperial Palace East Garden is a worthy consolation.

Stroll the Tranquil Palace Gardens

The **Imperial Palace East Garden** (MAP: P40 **B2**) makes up a large portion of the former Edo Castle

FREE GUIDED TOURS OF THE EAST GARDEN
Several volunteer organisations offer guided tours of the East Garden. My favourites are the guides working with Go Tokyo, who come well prepared with information about the garden and are very friendly. You will need to pay transport fees for you and your guides, but the cost is still very reasonable.

grounds. This part of the palace is open to the public free of charge and contains the site of the original Edo Castle keep. Not much remains of the structure now, but you can stand on the hill where it once stood and use your imagination as you survey the rest of the gardens.

The gardens are the perfect reprieve from the bustle of the city and can be absolutely stunning between spring and autumn, when seasonal flowers are used to highlight the beautifully manicured space. You can also enjoy watching the graceful koi swimming in the pond in the Ninomaru area, which were bred by the Emperor Emeritus. If you'd like to learn about the history of the structures found around the garden and Imperial Palace, download the free Imperial Palace audio-guide app.

Museum of Imperial Collections

The substantial collection of art gifted to the public by the Emperor Emeritus in 1989 is displayed in **Sannomaru Shōzōkan** (Museum of Imperial Collections; MAP: P40 **B2**; *shozokan.nich.go.jp, free*) near the entrance to the East Garden. The pieces are exemplary works of art and crafts representing various eras dating back to the 4th century. More contemporary works created by imperial court artists, such as paintings and sculptures, are also part of the collection, as well as pieces created by artists from other countries given as gifts of friendship to the Imperial Family. Note that the museum is closed until autumn 2026 for an expansion of the building.

WYNN WYGAL/SHUTTERSTOCK

Walk Nihombashi

To see how easily the present and the past mingle in Nihombashi, explore the area on foot. A mix of European-inspired classical buildings, glass and steel skyscrapers, and tiny family-run businesses sit comfortably together along cherry-tree-lined streets and Nihombashi-gawa.

START	END	LENGTH
Mitsukoshimae Station (Exit A7)	Nihonbashi Bridge	2km; 2hr

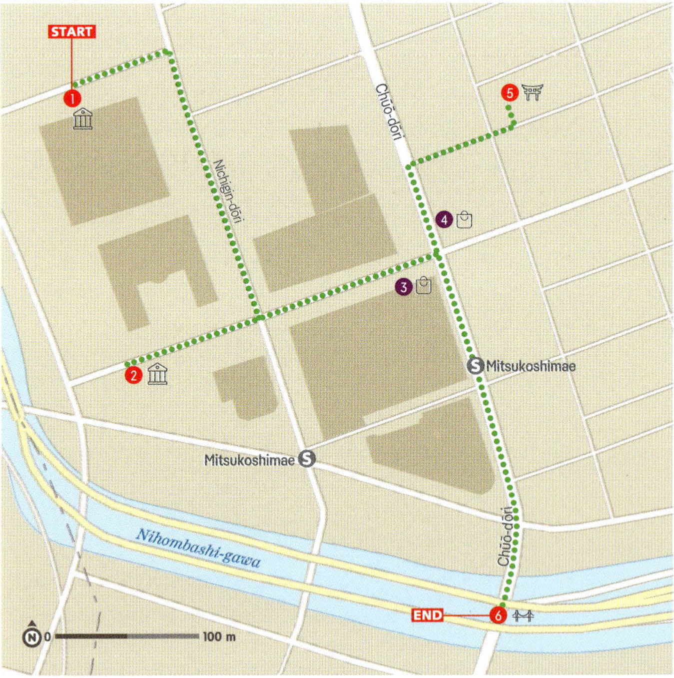

1 Nihombashi's European Architecture

Our first stop is the green-roofed **Bank of Japan Head Office**, an imposing European-style building by Tatsuno Kingo, who also designed Tokyo Station. On the third Wednesday of every month, you can take a guided tour in English with prior online reservation. Then, walk down Nichigin-dōri, flanked by the bank and the neo-classical **Mitsui Main Building**. Both are designated Important Cultural Properties.

2 Gold Coins & Cash

Continue down Nichigin-dōri and you'll come to the **Bank of Japan Currency Museum** (p48), which contains everything you've ever wanted to know about Japanese currency through the ages. Admission is free, and the exhibits are far more engaging than you'd imagine, with an English audio guide.

3 Historical Department Store

Just a block away is **Mitsukoshi** (p64), Japan's first department store. The boxy, European-style building is guarded by bronze lions at the entrance, and has a towering statue of Magokoro, the goddess of sincerity, in the atrium. The interior of the building retains a vintage vibe, but also a luminous area designed by architect Kengo Kuma. There's an art gallery on the 6th floor of the building.

4 Modern Architecture & Edo-Era Vibes

Across the main road is **Coredo Muromachi**, a shopping complex (three malls and a terrace) that incorporates Edo-era elements into its interior design, such as warm, natural woods and soft lighting. Shops are mainly focused on food and lifestyle, with an emphasis on Japanese design and cuisine.

5 Shrine of Lottery Tickets

Stroll down the lantern-lined street between the Coredo shopping malls and you'll come to a junction, where a *torii* (entrance gate) marks the entry to **Fukutoku-jinja**, an elegant Shintō shrine situated beneath a skyscraper that it predates by about 12 centuries. The shrine's unique history selling lottery tickets makes it a popular place to pray for a big win.

6 Japan's Bridge

Head back onto the main avenue and continue south towards the historic **Nihonbashi Bridge**. The original Nihonbashi was a large wooden bridge built in the Edo period, when it was the destination of all the major roads from around the nation, featured often in iconic *ukiyo-e* (woodblock prints). It's difficult to picture its grandeur in its current state, but the unsightly overhead expressway that hides it will be removed by 2041.

EXPERIENCES

Shop for 'Designed & Made in Japan' — SHOPPING

As the centre of the finest goods manufactured in Japan for centuries, it's quite easy to find many shops that still make and sell Japanese-designed goods around Nihombashi. The 220-year-old company **Haibara** (MAP: ① P40 **E3**; *haibara.co.jp*) resides in an elegant box-shaped store next door to Takashimaya department store's Nihombashi location, selling exquisitely designed handmade paper products and stationery. **Hario Lampwork Factory** (MAP: ② P40 **F1**; *hario-lwf.com*) has been crafting household goods from its main factory in Nihombashi for more than a century; drop by to purchase glass jewellery pieces and watch their skilled artisans at work. If you enjoy needlework, **Cohana** (MAP: ③ P40 **E1**; *cohana.style/en/store*) is a small Nihombashi shop selling its own brand of sewing pins, pincushions and sewing scissors that are highly functional in design and beautiful to the eye.

Cruise Tokyo's Ancient Waterways — CRUISE

Tokyo's site was chosen for its position on a protected bay fed by numerous wide rivers. Waterways were the primary method of travel long before the elevated expressways were built over them in the 1960s. See Tokyo via the waterways by hopping on a short river cruise departing Nihombashi, right near the bridge. Most tours range from 45 minutes to less than 2 hours and are affordably priced. Booking tickets in advance is always recommended, but you may also spot kiosks set up near the bridge selling same-day tickets.

All cruises have a tour guide, though they typically only speak Japanese. **Nihonbashi Cruise** (MAP: ④ P40 **E2**; *nihonbashi-cruise.jp*) organises cherry-blossom-viewing boat trips as well as night cruises, though tickets must be booked in advance. For a cosier experience aboard a smaller boat, make a reservation at **Riverboat Mizuha** (MAP: ⑤ P40 **E2**; *funaasobi-mizuha.jp*), which offers private charters too.

Have Bite-Sized Cultural Experiences — MUSEUMS

There are several small but excellent museums in the area that you can visit in just an hour or two. You don't even have to spend a single yen – some museums, like the **Bank of Japan Currency Museum** (MAP: ⑥ P40 **E2**; *imes.boj.or.jp/cm*), are free. This Nihombashi area museum houses a large collection of old coins, ingots and paper currency beginning from ancient times. There's another museum just a few steps away, the **Mitsui Memorial Museum** (MAP: ⑦ P40 **E2**; *mitsui-museum.jp; adult/child from ¥1200/free*), with its collection of fine works of Japanese and

Western art that have been acquired by the wealthy former merchant family.

Around Tokyo Station, don't miss **Intermediatheque** (MAP: **8** P40 **C3**; *intermediatheque. jp; free*) – a contemporary museum in the KITTE shopping mall that feels like it's part art gallery, part billionaire explorer's private collection, with rocks, skeletons, preserved insects and even mummies. The Tokyo Station Gallery (p41) is worth visiting too, as it takes you up to the 2nd floor of one of the domes in the station building otherwise inaccessible to the public.

Stroll under Winter Illuminations

SEASONAL SIGHTS

The highlight of the weeks leading up to Christmas is the glittering winter lights events that happen all around Tokyo, with those in Marunouchi being particularly beautiful. Between November and February, the trees lining Marunouchi Naka-dōri, which runs parallel to Tokyo Station on its west side, are strung up with 1.2 million fairy lights, giving the city a warm glow. It's the perfect setting for a romantic stroll, and when you need to escape the cold, the Christmas displays inside buildings such as the Marunouchi Building's Marucube atrium are worth checking out, too. If you have about an hour, you can stroll the length of the illuminations, passing Tokyo International Forum

KITTE'S BEST SHOPS
Former main post office turned shopping centre **KITTE** (MAP: **9** P40 **D3**; *jptower-kitte.jp*) is full of great shops, but here are the best among them:

Nakagawa Masashichi is a shop from Nara featuring modern Japanese-designed clothing, houseware and accessories.

Hacoa offers unique wooden products made from the forests of Fukui, transforming everyday items such as USB drives and business-card holders into works of art.

Good Design Store Tokyo by Nohara carries nearly 1000 lifestyle items that have been awarded Japan's Good Design Award.

Snow Peak sells high-quality camping goods and outdoor wear designed and made in Japan with a lifetime repair warranty.

to Yūrakuchō Station and back with plenty of time to warm up with a hot beverage along the way.

Drift along the Palace Moat

OUTDOOR ACTIVITY

MAP: **10** P40 **A1**

The best way to experience the beauty of the Edo Castle moat is on the water at **Chidori-ga-fuchi**.

Rowing boats are available for rent from spring to autumn, with the peak demand period from late March to early April when you'll glide under the falling petals of nearby cherry blossom trees. If no reservations are available during peak season, arrive early to queue for a ticket, which comes with a designated time-slot.

For two evenings in summer, the moat is filled with floating lanterns that bob alongside the boats. Opportunities to participate are limited, so your best bet is to enjoy the scene from the 700m-long path that snakes along the moat, where crowds gather to take photos of this atmospheric event.

If you visit Chidori-ga-fuchi outside of these two major events, you'll find it is quite a peaceful place to enjoy the simpler beauty of Tokyo.

Learn a Traditional Craft at Ozu Washi

HANDS-ON

MAP: **11** P40 **F1**

The folks at **Ozu Washi** *(ozuwashi. net; courses ¥1000-1500)* know a little about making paper; they've been doing it at this location in Nihombashi since 1653. Their shop carries a huge selection of beautiful handmade papers, but you can also experience what it's like to make your own unique creation.

Using mulberry fibre and a *sugeta* (paper mould), you can choose between a standard smooth piece of *washi* paper or a lace *washi,* where the paper is covered with a mould and thinned using a spray of water to create intricate patterns. Another option allows you to add coloured paper or dried flowers for a unique look.

Walk-ins are welcome if there's space, but there's a good chance the workshop will be booked solid weeks in advance, so make reservations to avoid disappointment. The workshop is 45 minutes long but plan to spend a little longer exploring the shop and a small history museum.

Best Places for...

❶ Budget   ❷❷ Midrange   ❸❸❸ Top End

Eating

Fine Dining

The Café
by Aman
❸❸❸

12 C2

Perfect for a casual date or just a bite to eat, hidden in a little forest outside the Aman Hotel. *aman.com/hotels/aman -tokyo/dining/cafe-aman; 11am-2.30pm lunch, 1-4pm dessert, 5-9pm dinner*

est ❸❸❸

13 C1

French cuisine is infused with Japanese flavours at this Michelin-starred restaurant, where ingredients are sourced locally and sustainably. On the 39th floor of the Four Seasons Hotel. *est-tokyo. com; noon-3pm & 6-10pm Tue-Sun*

Grill Ukai ❸❸❸

14 C4

Generously portioned and delicious lunch set overlooking the plaza of the Mitsubishi Ichigokan Museum. *ukai.co.jp/grill; 11.30am-3pm & 5.30-9.30pm Thu-Tue*

Historical Restaurants

Nihombashi
Izumoya ❷❷

15 E1

Serving delicious *unagi* (eel) since the 1940s, this restaurant is now run by the original owner's grandson, and all of the meals come in beautiful lacquer boxes. *idumoya. com; 11am-2pm & 5-9pm, Mon-Tue & Wed-Sat*

Janoichi Honten ❷❷

16 F2

Established in the late 1800s, this restaurant still serves classic Edomae sushi. Come for the lunchtime meals, offered at a reasonable price. *jyanoichi.tokyo; 11.30am-2pm & 4.30-10.30pm Mon-Sat*

Muromachi Sunaba ❶

17 E1

This historic restaurant, opened in 1869, invented *tenzaru* – soba noodles served with a side of tempura. *muromachi -sunaba.co.jp/nihonbashi;*

11.30am-9pm Mon-Fri, to 4pm Sat

Momijigawa ❷❷

18 E2

Traditional soba noodle restaurant across from Mitsukoshi department store offering a rustic duck soba. *11am-2.30pm & 5-8.30pm Mon-Fri, 11-3pm Sat-Sun*

Gyukatsu
Motomura ❷❷

19 E1

Deep-fried breaded beef cutlets popular since just after the Edo period. The Nihombashi branch in Coredo Muromachi isn't as busy as those in other parts of Tokyo. *gyukatsu -motomura.com/shop/ coredo-muromachi; 11am-9pm*

Sweet Treats

Fruit Parlour
Kajitsuen ❷❷

20 D3

Parfaits piled high with strawberries and other seasonal fruit, plus beautiful fruit cakes. Inside Tokyo Station, but beyond the turnstiles. *kajitsuen. jp; 11am-9pm*

Sembikiya Fruit Parlour 

21 E1

A fruit store in the Edo period, Sembikiya is now a chain of fruit cafes known for its luxury produce. Its famous musk melon is available year-round. *sembikiya.co.jp; 11am-9pm*

Harbs 

22 C3

At this branch in the Marunouchi Building is an enormous menu of cakes that changes regularly with seasonal ingredients. *harbs.co.jp; 11am-8pm*

Coco Gelato 

23 E1

Tiny shop near Fukutoku Shrine sells regionally inspired flavours of gelato. *11am-8pm*

Usagiya Nihonbashi 

24 E2

A no-frills traditional sweets store selling delicious *dorayaki* (red-bean pancakes). It was established in 1948 by the son of the original founder of Usagiya in Ueno, though the recipe is said to be different. *9.30am-6pm Mon-Fri*

Drinking

Cocktails & Craft Beer

Hitachino Brewing

25 D3

A spacious bar on the Yaesu side of Tokyo Station for enjoying a few rounds of Hitachino's craft beers from Ibaraki Prefecture. *kodawari.cc/ restaurant/brewing.html; 10am-10pm Mon-Sat, to 9pm Sun*

Mandarin Bar

26 E1

This luxury hotel bar has it all: sleek and stylish decor, stunning views from the 37th-floor windows, and out-of-this-world cocktails heavy on the Japanese influences. *mandarinoriental.com/ en/tokyo/nihonbashi; 3pm-midnight Mon-Fri, from noon Sat-Sun*

Virtù

27 C1

Classy but not snobby, this 39th-floor bar of the Four Seasons Hotel provides excellent service and an elegant atmosphere. *fourseasons .com/otemachi/dining/ restaurants/virtu;*

5pm-midnight Sun-Wed, to 12.30am Thu-Sat

Heiwa Doburoku Kabutocho

28 F3

Once considered the 'moonshine' liquor of Japan, *doburoku*, a fizzy, cloudy version of sake, is given a polish at this unique Nihombashi bar. *heiwashuzou.co.jp/ heiwa-doburoku- kabutocho; 1-10.30pm Mon-Fri, noon-10.30pm Sat, noon-9pm Sun*

Tea Rooms

Wang De Chuan

29 E1

Premium Taiwanese oolong teas served hot and fragrant or cold with a foamy top. Inside the Eslite Spectrum Nihonbashi bookstore. *dechuantea.com; 11am-7pm Mon-Fri, to 8pm Sat-Sun*

Ippuku & Matcha

30 E1

The menu here is entirely comprised of matcha offerings, including matcha-infused desserts. Mostly takeouts, but you can also reserve a spot in the special tea room. *ippukuandmatcha.jp; 11am-8pm*

Tsuruya Yoshinobu Tokyo Mise

 **31** E1

The Tokyo location of a renowned Japanese sweets-maker from Kyoto. The delicate confections pair perfectly with a strong cup of matcha. *tsuruyayoshinobu.jp/shop /tokyo-mise; 11am-8pm Mon-Fri, from 10am Sat-Sun*

Unique Cafes

Bongen Coffee

32 E4

Strong cups of coffee, espresso and matcha lattes in one of the most Zen cafes you've ever seen. *bongen-shira fushi-coffee.com; 10am-5pm*

Good Coffee Farms Cafe

33 E3

Single-origin, farm-to-cup coffee and a selection of sweets in a no-frills coffee shop. Customers get a card showing the farmer who produced the beans for their coffee. *goodcoffeefarms.com; 8am-5pm*

Aroma Coffee Yaesu

34 E3

Kissaten-style coffee shop with a reasonably priced morning set for early risers. Underground in the Yaechika shopping mall. *7am-9.30pm Mon-Fri, 7am-9pm Sat, 7.30am-9pm Sun*

Bridge Coffee & Ice Cream

 **35** F1

Great single-origin hand-drip coffee, deep espresso and rich ice cream in six flavours are served in an iconic blue-tiled Nihom-bashi building. *brdg. jp; 8am-7pm Mon-Fri, 9am-7pm Sat-Sun*

Shopping

Sweets & Condiments

Kayanoya

 **36** E2

This beautiful shop selling premium *shōyu* (soy sauce) and *dashi* (stock) was designed by Kengo Kuma and has wooden barrels hanging from the ceiling. *kayanoya.com/ en/shop/nihonbashi; 11am-8pm Mon-Fri, from 10am Sat-Sun*

Eitaro Sohonpo Nihombashi

37 E2

Established in 1818, this well-loved confectionery shop produces traditional sweets and snacks from the Edo era beautifully packaged to give as unique gifts. *eitarosou honpo.co.jp; 10am-5pm Mon-Sat*

Arts & Crafts

Kuroeya

38 E2

A traditional lacquerware shop in business for over 300 years where you'll find homeware and design products for serious collectors along with affordable bowls and cups you can use daily. *kuroeya.com; 9am-6pm Mon-Fri*

Ōedo Antique Market

39 C4

Approximately twice a month, this large antique market is held in the courtyard of the Tokyo International Forum with about 250 vendors selling quality antique goods. Check the website for the latest schedule as it is subject to change. *antique-market.jp; 9am-4pm, some vendors leave early*

See p65
for eating,
drinking and
shopping
listings

極
本

HOTEL TOKYU STAY

築地 すし一番

24 時間営業 すぐヨコ

人情味溢れ
築地場外

うおがし丼
電話03-3546-0300

井上

豊吉(卸)
821-5759

KANNO
Sushi Cafe

Explore
Ginza & Tsukiji

Researched by
Todd Fong

Home to luxury-brand flagship stores, stylish cafes and contemporary art galleries by day, and swanky cocktail bars and fine restaurants by night, Ginza (銀座) has long been the destination for those wishing to part with their cash in extravagant ways. Yet Ginza still holds pleasant surprises, even for those on a budget. Nearby Tsukiji (築地) is the former home of Tokyo's energetic fish market, but although it has moved to a sparkly new facility across the water, tourists still prefer the raw authenticity of Tsukiji's outer market with its dozens of restaurants selling fresh seafood and other delicacies.

Getting Around

 **Train**

On the JR Yamanote line, the closest stations to Ginza are Shimbashi Station and Yūra-kuchō Station.

 **Metro**

Ginza Station is closest to the main shopping area and is connected to the Ginza, Hibiya and Marunouchi lines. Kabuki-za theatre is accessible via Higashi-ginza Station on the Hibiya and Asakusa lines. Tsukiji Station on the Hibiya Line is the closest to the outer market, while Tsukijishijō on the Ōedo Line is also nearby.

 **Walk**

Ginza and Tsukiji are within a 20-minute walk of each other.

THE BEST

CULTURAL EXPERIENCE
Kabuki-za (p57)

CAFE LATTE
Turret Coffee (p66)

SOUVENIR SHOPPING
Cibone Case (p67)

FREE MUSEUM
Seiko Museum (p63)

JAPANESE GARDENS
Hama-rikyū
Onshi-teien (p59)

Tsukiji Outer Market (p64)

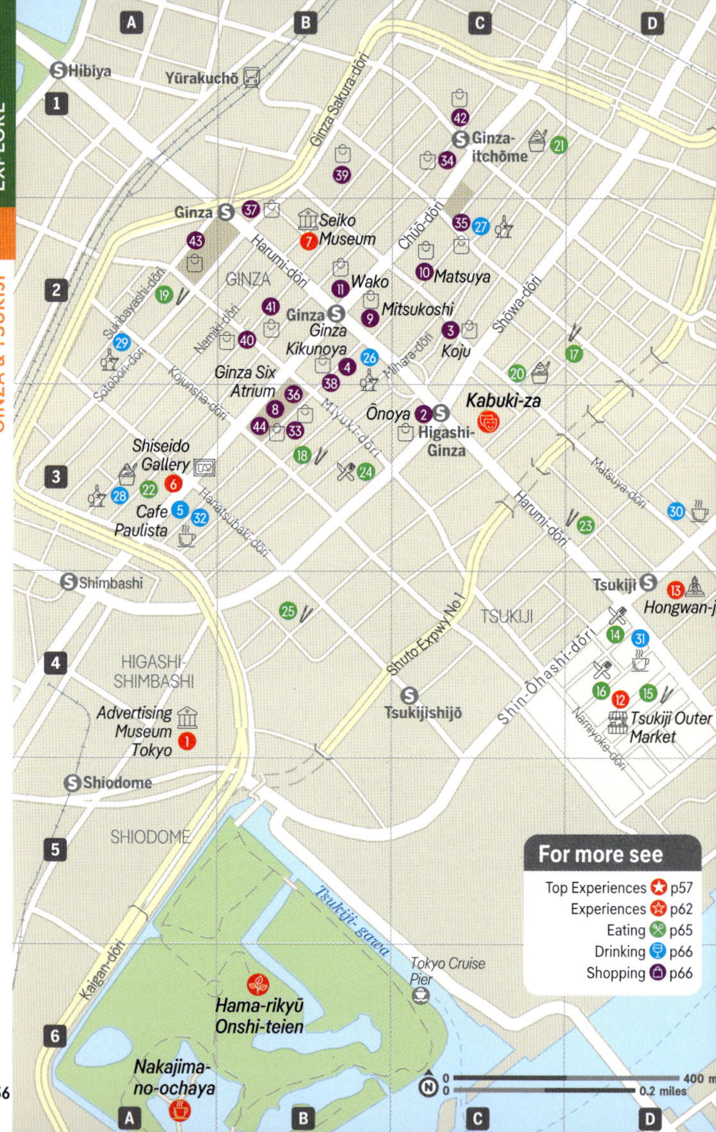
A
B
C
D
1
2
3
4
5
6

Hibiya
Yūrakuchō
42
Ginza-itchōme
21
34
39
Ginza
37
43
19
Seiko Museum
7
35
27
GINZA
11
Wako
10
Matsuya
41
Ginza
9
Mitsukoshi
40
Ginza Kikunoya
3
Koju
4
26
38
17
20
Kabuki-za
36
Ginza Six Atrium
8
Ōnoya
2
44
33
Higashi-Ginza
Shiseido Gallery
18
24
28
22
6
Cafe Paulista
5
32
30
Shimbashi
25
Tsukiji
13
Hongwan-j
TSUKIJI
14
31
HIGASHI-SHIMBASHI
16
12
15
Advertising Museum Tokyo
1
Tsukijishijō
Tsukiji Outer Market
Shiodome
SHIODOME
For more see
Top Experiences p57
Experiences p62
Eating p65
Drinking p66
Shopping p66
Tsukiji-gawa
Tokyo Cruise Pier
Hama-rikyū Onshi-teien
Nakajima-no-ochaya
N
0
400 m
0
0.2 miles
Ginza Sakura-dōri
Harumi-dōri
Chūō-dōri
Shōwa-dōri
Mihara-dōri
Miyuki-dōri
Namiki-dōri
Kōjunsha-dōri
Sotobori-dōri
Sukibayashi-dōri
Hanatsubaki-dōri
Matsuya-dōri
Harumi-dōri
Shuto Expwy No.1
Shin-Ōhashi-dōri
Namiyoke-dōri
Kaigan-dōri

⭐ **TOP EXPERIENCE**

Kabuki-za

Everything about kabuki theatre is truly a spectacle – from the actors' dramatically painted faces to their beautiful costumes, exaggerated movements and elaborate stagecraft. Dating back to the 17th century as a popular form of folk entertainment, the art form still has a hold on the population today – and Ginza's Kabuki-za *(kabukiweb.net)* is where to see it all happen.

MAP P56 **C3**

A Grand Affair

For many a Tokyoite, attending a performance at Kabuki-za is an opportunity to don a fine kimono, eat an extravagant meal and enjoy a show featuring a favourite actor. Even the building itself, renovated to recreate its design from 1924, is more than a little fancy. The performances themselves, however, were written for the masses and were one of the most popular forms of entertainment for the common people of Edo.

The Theatre

With its sloped roofs and grand facade adorned with red lanterns and towering banners, Kabu-ki-za is an outlier in Ginza's more modern, urban landscape. Though it was first built in 1889, the building has gone through several iterations after previous structures were lost due to natural disasters and fires.

The History of Kabuki

When kabuki was invented in 17th-century Kyoto, the troupes were mainly women. Morality laws eventually banned them from the stage in 1652 and from then on, kabuki has been the realm of men.

PLANNING TIP
A full kabuki performance lasts several hours, but visitors have the option to catch a single act. Purchase tickets in advance online or try your luck on the day.

Scan this QR code for information about purchasing single-act kabuki tickets.

JAPAN POOL/JIJI PRESS/AFP VIA GETTY IMAGES

QUICK BREAK
Getting a *bentō* to eat during intermission is part of the theatre-going experience. There are a few options available on the basement floor of the theatre.

Donning wigs and kimonos, men portray women on stage, training from a young age to perfect every movement and intonation.

Kabuki performances are often based on dramatised historic events or legendary tales, but recently performances based on anime have been very successful.

Enjoying Kabuki for First-Timers

Many first-timers want to ease their way into kabuki with a single-act ticket (*¥500-8000*). But if you are motivated to see an entire performance, don't be intimidated. English captioning devices detailing the play synopsis and key dialogue are available to rent and regular seats offer better views of the costumes, backgrounds and actors' performances.

Hama-rikyū Onshi-teien

One of Tokyo's most idyllic spots, Hama-rikyū Onshi-teien is a refuge from the bustle of the city, where an afternoon involves weaving your way around pine trees and manicured lawns or enjoying a cup of tea while feeling the sea breeze that drifts from nearby Tokyo Bay.

MAP P56 **B6**

Scenic Gardens

Hama-rikyū Onshi-teien was established by the Tokugawa shogunate, whose members enjoyed it as a hunting ground. The garden came under possession of the Imperial Family until 1945, when it was donated to the City of Tokyo. Buildings from nearby Shiodome rise above the park's tree line; the juxtaposition makes for beautiful photographs of an urban oasis. Within the park are several reflective ponds, the largest being Shiori-no-ike.

PLANNING TIP
You can walk here after a trip to Tsukiji Market, or take the scenic route and come here by boat from Asakusa.

Teahouses

It could take over an hour of strolling along the paths to see the entire garden, but you'll come across several teahouses along the way. Stop by **Nakajima-no-ochaya** (MAP P56 **A6**) for a cup of matcha and *wagashi* (Japanese sweets). It sits in the middle of Shiori-no-ike, with a deck that provides an unobstructed view of the gardens from the water.

Autumn for the Best Views

Although Japanese gardens are designed to be beautiful in all seasons, Tokyo gardens suffer from a lack of snow and often just appear dull during the winter months. Hama-rikyū seems to have been optimised for autumn, with colourful ginkgo and maple trees announcing the season with brightly coloured leaves.

Scan this QR code for detailed information about the garden.

Walk Ginza

A walk through Ginza is simultaneously a lesson in contemporary architecture, cutting-edge fashion and the past coexisting with the present. Among the flagship stores and effortlessly fashionable people you'll discover small establishments that have been doing business here for over 150 years.

START	END	LENGTH
Kabuki-za	L'ibisco	2km; 2hr

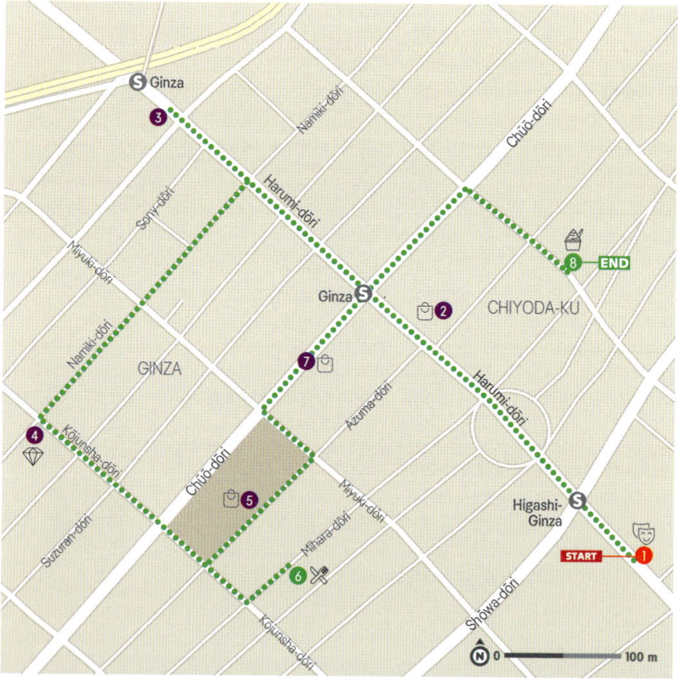

1 The Kabuki Theatre

Begin your journey at Higashi-ginza Station, which sits just below **Kabuki-za** (p57). Descend to the basement level to browse the theatre's excellent gift shop. Head back outside and snap pictures of the grand, classic facade and beautiful painted show posters on display.

2 Ginza's Icons

Walk up Harumi-dōri towards the swanky part of Ginza. At the intersection of Harumi-dōri and Chūō-dōri are three icons: **Mitsukoshi** (p64), whose flagship in Nihombashi was Japan's first department store; **Nissan Crossing** showroom with its futuristic latticed structure, and the **Wako** department store (p64), whose clocktower is a symbol of Ginza.

3 Little Shibuya Crossing

Continuing along Harumi-dōri, you will reach the newly constructed brutalist Ginza Sony Park public space at **Sukibayashi Crossing**, Ginza's answer to the more famous Shibuya Crossing. The glass cathedral-like **Tokyu Plaza** shopping centre is on the opposite side.

4 Avant-Garde Architecture

Double back slightly and head south on Namiki-dōri, passing more examples of Ginza's impressive modern architecture: the glass blocks of **Hermès Ginza** and the stark black-and-white tower of the **Chanel** building, eventually arriving at the jellyfish-like **Louis Vuitton** store at Kōjunsha-dōri.

5 An Artsy Mall

Turn right on Kōjunsha-dōri and continue until you arrive at **Ginza Six** (p63), a mall full of shops that are fun to browse. Check out **Gyokusendō** for traditional copperware and **Tsutaya Books** (p66) for a huge collection of art books.

6 Take a Ramen Break

Duck behind the Ginza Six building to find **Mugi to Olive** (p65), a ramen shop consistently winning awards for its clam-based broth and thin noodles. There's often a queue, but it's worth the wait.

7 Main Street Ginza

Weekends and public holidays are the best for a stroll, when pedestrians are given full reign of **Chūō-dōri**, the wide avenue that is Ginza's main shopping street. Lining it are more department stores, luxury boutiques and speciality stores – some of which date back to the early days of the neighbourhood, such as its first department store, **Matsuya** (p64) and popular stationery emporium **Itōya** (p67).

8 A Sweet Ending

Finish your Ginza tour with a sweet treat – freshly made gelato from **L'ibisco** (p65), just a couple of blocks off the main street. It's a bit hidden on the second floor of a shop on the corner.

EXPERIENCES

Find the Truth in Japanese Advertising
MUSEUM

MAP: **1** P56 **A4**

Any visitor to Japan knows you can't escape the advertisements – on oversized video billboards, screens on subways and trains, and even in 10-second elevator rides. At **Advertising Museum Tokyo** (*admt.jp; free),* you'll learn how the Japanese have been perfecting the art for over three centuries.

This unconventional museum is the work of Dentsu, Japan's largest advertising agency. It chronicles the history of advertising in Japan, starting from 1673 with Mitsui Takatoshi, founder of Echigoya, which would eventually become Japan's first department store, Mitsukoshi. Using cutting-edge marketing techniques and eventually leveraging the power of woodblock printing, Mitsui used advertising to create excitement around his products.

The museum has a digital and print collection of over 320,000 materials, from ancient woodblocks to modern video clips, giving a comprehensive look at Japan's advertising over the centuries. It's a fascinating way to see the evolution of Japanese culture and society alongside the historical context of regime changes, wars and prosperity. Best of all, admission to the museum is free.

Discover Ginza's Traditional Side
SHOPPING

With all the glitz and glamour, it's easy to forget that Ginza has a traditional side too. Many traditional Japanese crafts are represented in this neighbourhood by long-established businesses, as well as food and drink establishments that have been loved for well over a century.

At a busy intersection near Kabuki-za, **Ōnoya** (MAP: **2** P56 **C3**; *ginza-oonoya.com*) is an original Ginza shop dealing in traditional *tabi* socks, *tenugui* hand towels and other textile-related goods. The company has been making *tabi* for nearly 170 years and counts kabuki actors among its many customers.

Nearby **Koju** (MAP: **3** P56 **C2**; *koju. co.jp*) is easily missed as the main part of the shop is underground. Although not local to Ginza, this 400-year-old Kyoto company producing incense and other aromatic goods sells many unique items that will bring back fond memories of Japan.

For something sweet, **Ginza Kikunoya** (MAP: **4** P56 **B2**; *ginza-kikunoya.co.jp*) is a confectionery store synonymous with Ginza from its humble beginnings selling *sembei* rice crackers to kabuki performance attendees. Today, the shop sells traditional sweets and crackers in adorable tins that make perfect Ginza-themed gifts.

Sip Coffee at a Kissaten CAFES

MAP: **5** P56 **A3**

Kissaten ('tea-drinking shop') is a bit of a misnomer. These Japanese-style cafes that first came into popularity during the early 20th century usually specialise in coffee and still instill a sense of nostalgia in the hearts of many a Tokyoite. Trendy Ginza was where some of the city's earliest *kissaten* first appeared, featuring warm, cosy, lamp-lit interiors – a style that is still synonymous with *kissaten* today.

Founded in the 1910s, the venerable **Cafe Paulista** *(paulista. co.jp),* is said to be the oldest *kissaten* still in business. Like many other *kissaten,* Cafe Paulista offers a light lunch menu that includes toast, sandwiches and European-style dishes called *yōshoku,* which include *omurice* (tomato fried rice topped with a runny omelette) and the sweet, ketchup-based spaghetti Napolitan. But if all you crave is a pick-me-up cup of joe or a refreshing affogato, late afternoons are the least busy times.

Explore Ginza's Department Stores SHOPPING

Visiting a Japanese department store is a cultural experience unto itself. Arrive when the doors open for an iconic sight of Japanese *omotenashi* hospitality – staff and management lined up to greet customers with a deep bow.

FREE ART IN GINZA

Art has always been a part of Ginza's DNA so it is no surprise you can find museums, galleries and exhibitions everywhere, many of them for free.

Shiseido Gallery The sleek basement gallery of the Japanese cosmetic company displays the work of contemporary artists.
MAP: **6** P56 **A3**

Seiko Museum This surprisingly comprehensive museum features the art and beauty of Seiko timepieces over the history of the company.
MAP: **7** P56 **B2**

Ginza Six Atrium You can often find contemporary art suspended over and in the rest areas surrounding the large multistorey atrium of this chic shopping mall.
MAP: **8** P56 **B3**

Most department stores are made up of their own departments mixed with small private boutique shops that change regularly to generate new interest in the store. Department categories are often divided by floors, with women's items taking up the lower levels, and lifestyle goods and toys on the upper floors. The goods are usually sandwiched between the food, with fashionable sit-down restaurants on the top floor or floors and the *depachika*, a floor dedicated to beautifully displayed desserts, prepared foods and food-related gifts, on the basement level.

Ginza has three department stores: **Mitsukoshi** (MAP: 9 P56 **B2**); **Matsuya** (MAP: 10 P56 **C2**) and **Wako** (MAP: 11 P56 **B2**). Mitsukoshi's unique feature is the **Art Aquarium Museum** located on the 9th floor, while Wako is famous for its collection of fine watches.

Eat & Shop Tsukiji Outer Market
DINING & SHOPPING

Many believed the relocation of Tokyo's largest fish market in 2018 from Tsukiji to Toyosu would spell the end of this historically popular location, but the authentic vibe and long-established shops that remained after the market left keep drawing crowds of tourists and to a lesser extent, locals who know their way around the shops and restaurants.

Most visitors come to **Tsukiji Outer Market** (MAP: 12 P56 **D4**; *tsukiji.or.jp*) to eat. There's a collection of street-food vendors and sit-down restaurants, although the latter tend to be priced more for the tourists. Take your time to shop around and you may find some good deals, however.

Most shops are food-related: Japanese pickled products, dried seaweed and kitchenware such as knives and tableware. For shopping, plan to arrive and finish early; most shops open around or before dawn and close by 2 or 3pm. Many are closed on Sundays and some Wednesdays.

But Tsukiji is not just about the market. Nearby **Hongwan-ji** (MAP: 13 P56 **D4**; *tsukijihongwanji. jp*) is a large Buddhist temple that relocated to Tsukiji in 1657. Its unique Indian-influenced architecture and eclectic interior design elements deserve a closer look.

CORNERSTONES OF GINZA

The anchors of Ginza are certainly the grand department stores, which have drawn crowds even from beyond the city limits to this glamorous neighbourhood for a century. **Matsuya** was the first Ginza department store to arrive in 1925 after starting life as a humble Yokohama kimono shop in 1869. **Mitsukoshi** followed in 1930, although it traces its roots back to 1683 with a small kimono shop in neighbouring Nihombashi, now the site of the Mitsukoshi main store. Lastly, **Wako** came in 1952, taking over the headquarters of K Hattori, better known as Seiko. Wako paid homage to the original owners by renaming the building Seiko House Ginza following renovations in 2022.

Best Places for...

❤Budget   ❤❤Midrange   ❤❤❤Top End

Eating

Tsukiji's Best Eats

Aji no Hamatō ❤

 **14** **D4**

The best fried-food-on-a-stick within the Tsukiji Outer Market. The small stand in front of the main shop has all kinds of *hanpen* (fishcakes) on display. *hamato.co.jp; 8am-3pm*

Sushi Sei ❤❤

15 **D4**

Sashimi bowls and sushi sets that are reasonably priced for its location in Tsukiji Outer Market. The staff are friendly and helpful with non-Japanese speakers. *tsuki jisushisay.co.jp; 11am-3pm & 5.30-9.30pm Mon-Fri, 11am-9.30pm Sat-Sun*

Yamachō ❤

16 **D4**

This Tsukiji market stall doles out juicy, golden *tamago-yaki* (omelette) on a stick, made fresh and piping hot. The queue may look daunting but it moves quickly. *6am-3.30pm*

Classy Ramen

Ginza Hachigō ❤

17 **D2**

Ramen broth here is loaded with umami derived from a blend of chicken, duck, mushroom and shellfish. Simple and delicious. *katsumoto -japan.com/en/ginza _hachigou; 11am-4pm Wed-Sun*

Mugi to Olive ❤❤

18 **B3**

This modest ramen shop frequently wins awards for the rich flavours of its chicken-clam broth and firm noodles. *11am-3.30pm & 5.30-9.30pm Thu-Tue*

Kagari Honten ❤❤

19 **A2**

The signature dish is a bowl of soba noodles in a thick chicken-based broth presented in a style worthy of one of those fancy stars. *11am-9.30pm*

Cakes & Sweet Treats

L'ibisco ❤

20 **C2**

Fresh gelato with delightful flavours like royal milk tea and matcha, plus seasonal offerings such as white peach and mandarin. *libisco.com; 11am-7pm*

Louange Tokyo Le Musée ❤❤❤

21 **C1**

One of Ginza's most extraordinary places to enjoy afternoon tea. But don't try to walk in; you'll likely need a reservation at least a day ahead. *louange-tokyo.com; 11am-9pm*

Shiseido Parlour Salon de Café ❤❤

22 **A3**

Amazing parfaits in the restaurant or tins of exquisite cookies from the shop. *parlour.shiseido. co.jp; 11am-9pm Tue-Sat 11am-8pm Sun*

Japanese Soul Foods

Nunotsune Sarashina ❤❤

23 **D3**

This historic shop for fresh soba noodles fills

up fast once it opens, but it's worth the wait for its richly flavoured broth. *11.30am-2pm & 5-8pm Tue-Fri, 11.30am-2pm Sat*

Kushiyaki Bistro Fukumimi 

24 B3

The Ginza location of this *yakitori* (skewer) restaurant got so popular, the owners opened another location a few blocks away. *4-11.25pm, closed holidays*

Chikuyotei Honten 

25 B4

One of the sweet secrets of this 100-year-old *unagi* (eel) restaurant is the private rooms available overlooking the restaurant's private garden. Attentive English-speaking staff. *g201101. gorp.jp; 11.30am-3.30pm & 4.30-9.30pm Mon-Sat*

Drinking

Ginza Cocktail Bars

Tír na nÓg

26 B2

Basement bar and cafe that can only be described as otherworldly. Lots of inventive drinks and cocktails. *tirnanog-ginza.com; cafe 11am-5pm, bar 5pm-4am*

Punch Room

27 C2

This bar at the Tokyo Ginza Edition makes a splash with signature punches with a Japanese twist. *editionhotels.com/ tokyo-ginza/restaurants -and-bars/punch-room; 6pm-midnight Tue-Thu, 6pm-2am Fri-Sat*

Bar Butler

28 A3

Consistently high-quality cocktails made by consummate professionals. *butler-gr.com; 5pm-2am Mon-Fri, 5pm-midnight Sat*

Little Smith

29 A2

Curved lofty ceilings and an oval bar that wraps around a pillar make this one of Ginza's most interesting bars. There's no menu here – order whatever you fancy. *little smith-english.chat-noir. co.jp; 6pm-3am Mon-Fri, 6pm-1am Sat*

Best Coffee

Turret Coffee

30 D3

Start the morning with a signature double-shot latte at this Tsukiji coffee shop that's considered one of the city's best. *7am-5pm Mon-Tue & Fri-Sat, 7am-3pm Thu, 8am-4pm Sun*

Yonemoto Coffee

31 D4

Friendly staff and delicious coffee at this Tsukiji coffee shop enjoyed by John Lennon and Yoko Ono. *yonemoto-coffee. com; 7.30am-3.30pm Sun-Fri, 7.30am-4pm Sat*

Café de l'Ambre

32 A3

Founded by single-minded coffee innovator Ichiro Sekiguchi. Come to this Ginza cafe for the perfect cup of coffee and nothing more. *11am-8pm Tue-Sat, 11am-6pm Sun*

Shopping

Lifestyle Goods

Ginza Tsutaya Books

33 B3

You could burn an entire day browsing the 60,000-plus art-related tomes in this fashionable bookstore that also stocks a curated stylish set of lifestyle goods. In Ginza Six. *store.tsite.jp/ ginza; 10.30am-9pm*

Kurashi-no-Kaori

34 C1

Minimalist-living and personal-care products with single-scent fragrances inspired by the seasons and traditions of Japan, such as cedar, green tea and yuzu. *kurashinokaori.com; 11.30am-8pm*

Itōya

35 C2

A century-old stationery shop on Chūō-dōri with multiple floors stocking all manner of cards, pens, inks, notebooks and souvenirs. Look for the giant red paperclip marking its storefront. *ito-ya.co.jp; 10am-8pm, to 7pm Sun*

Cibone Case

36 B3

Lifestyle-goods shop bringing together the best of Japanese-designed and -produced products from around Japan. A perfect stop for unique souvenirs in Ginza Six. *cibone.com; 10.30am-8.30pm*

Sanrio Nishiginza

37 B2

The ultra-*kawaii* (cute) brand's flagship store (and largest in the world) carries every conceivable iteration of Hello Kitty and her adorable friends.

stores.sanrio.co.jp/ 1703100; 11am-8pm

Fashion

Kindal Ginza

38 B2

You'd be forgiven for mistaking this second-hand brand-name goods shop for a boutique, with its well-designed interior and spotless used items on display. *kind.co.jp; 10am-8pm*

Muji Ginza

39 B1

Fans of minimalist design will have a field day inside Muji's flagship store, where beautiful displays show off everything from clothes to gadgets to pre-packaged foods. *shop.muji.com/jp/ginza; 11am-9pm*

Dover Street Market

40 B2

Seven floors of art and fashion make up this high-end retail store stocked with urban brands such as Comme des Garçons and A Bathing Ape. *ginza. doverstreetmarket.com; 11am-8pm*

Japanese Food & Drink

Uogashi Meicha

41 B2

The secret to the high-quality teas produced by this nearly-a-century-old tea seller is the fact it owns its tea fields and directly manages its shops. *uogashi-meicha.co.jp; 12 noon-7pm Tue-Sat*

Hiroshima TAU

42 C1

The next best thing to visiting Hiroshima, this 'antenna shop' stocks a huge variety of Hiroshima's famous goods and even has a Hiroshima-style *okonomiyaki* (savoury pancake) restaurant upstairs. *tau-hiroshima.jp; 10.30am-8pm*

Kuzefuku & Co

43 A2

Salad dressings, jams, pickles, miso, *dashi* (stock) and every sauce, spice and garnish imaginable are all on display here. In Tokyu Plaza Ginza. *kuzefuku.com; 11am-9pm*

Imadeya

44 B3

Take your time picking out a bottle of sake, *shōchū* or whatever spirit you might fancy from the shelves at this elegant bottle shop in the basement of Ginza Six. *imadeya.co.jp; 10am-8.30pm*

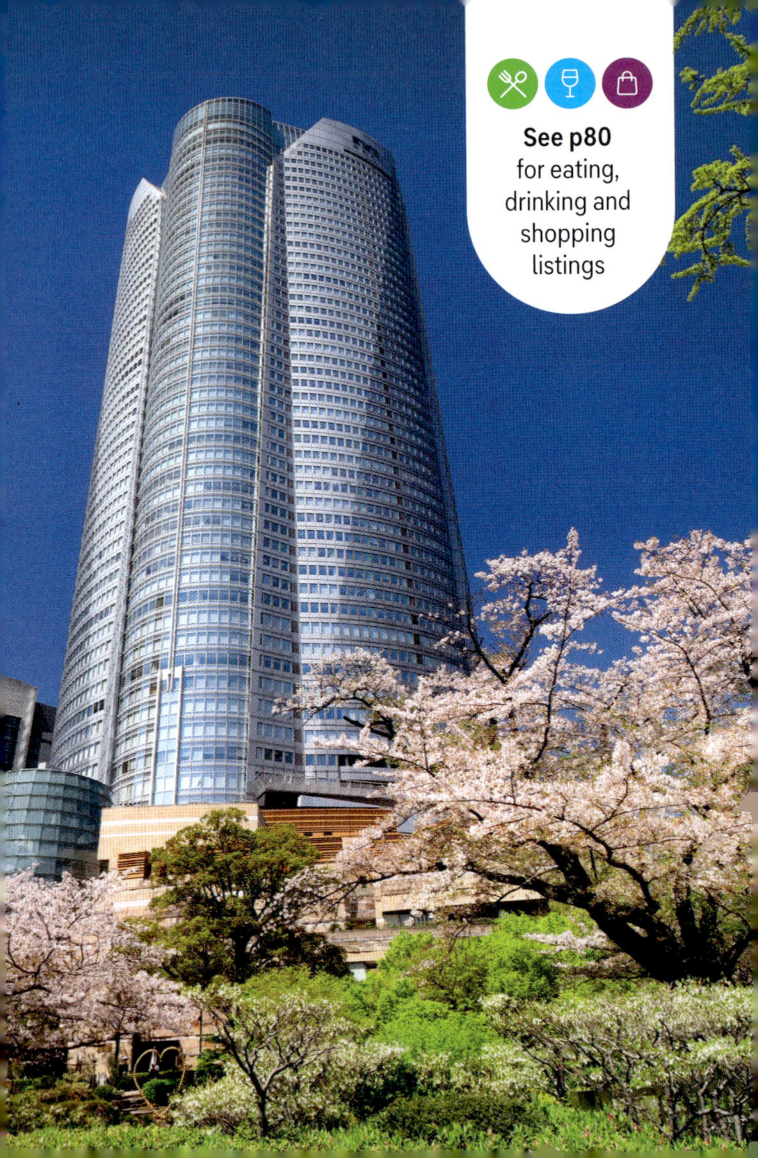
See p80
for eating,
drinking and
shopping
listings

Explore

Researched by Kim Kahan

Roppongi & Around

The Roppongi (六本木) area has undergone one of the most dramatic redevelopments in modern Tokyo history: once synonymous with uninhibited nightlife, it's now a world-class destination for art, design, dining and retail, dotted with 'mixed-use' complexes. The first post-modern mega malls, Roppongi Hills (2003) and Tokyo Midtown (2007), laid the groundwork for two more in 2023: innovation hub Toranomon Hills and Azabudai Hills, home to teamLab's signature digital art museum. Other neighbourhoods worth checking out include upscale residential district Azabu-jūban (麻布十番) and Akasaka (赤坂), a lively spot teeming with old-school bars. Meanwhile, the heart of Roppongi's nightlife district still beats around Roppongi Crossing.

Getting Around

 Metro

The area is well-connected to the Tokyo Metro. Stations include Roppongi Station, which joins to the Ōedo and Hibiya lines, Akasaka (Chiyoda and Ginza) and Toranomon (Ginza).

Walking

The Roppongi area is hilly but extremely walkable. It's around 20 to 25 minutes from Roppongi Crossing to either Azabudai, Toranomon or Akasaka.

Bicycle

Cycle-sharing apps such as Hello Cycling (credit card required) are easy to use around Roppongi's tarmacked roads. You might hit significant foot traffic in built-up areas, though, so be warned!

Mori Tower, Roppongi Hills (p73)

THE BEST

DIGITAL ART SPACE
teamLab Borderless (p72)

CONTEMPORARY ART CENTRE Mori Art Museum (p73)

SHOPPING
Tokyo Midtown (p76)

HISTORIC NEIGHBOURHOOD
Azabu-jūban (p76)

LOCAL LANDMARK
Tokyo Tower (p78)

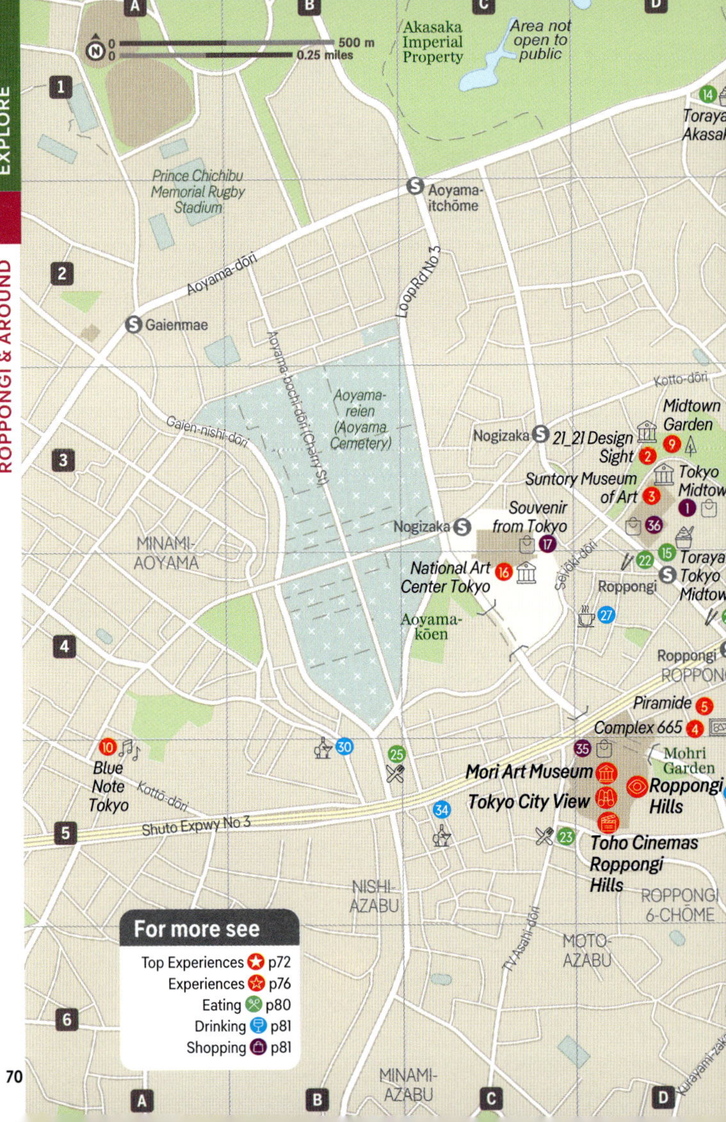

EXPLORE
ROPPONGI & AROUND
N
0   500 m
0   0.25 miles
Akasaka Imperial Property
Area not open to public
Toraya Akasak
14
Prince Chichibu Memorial Rugby Stadium
Aoyama-itchōme
Aoyama-dōri
Loop Rd No 3
Gaienmae
Aoyama-bochi-dōri (Cherry St)
Gaien-nishi-dōri
Aoyama-reien (Aoyama Cemetery)
Kotto-dōri
Midtown Garden
Nogizaka
21_21 Design Sight
2
9
Suntory Museum of Art
Tokyo Midtow
3
1
MINAMI-AOYAMA
Nogizaka
Souvenir from Tokyo
17
36
22 15
Toraya Tokyo Midtow
National Art Center Tokyo
16
Seijōki-dōri
Roppongi
Aoyama-kōen
27
Roppongi
2
Roppongi
ROPPONG
Piramide
5
Complex 665
4
Blue Note Tokyo
10
30
35
Mohri Garden
25
Mori Art Museum
Tokyo City View
Roppongi Hills
Kottō-dōri
Shuto Expwy No 3
34
Toho Cinemas Roppongi Hills
23
NISHI-AZABU
TV-Asahi-dōri
ROPPONGI 6-CHŌME
MOTO-AZABU
For more see
Top Experiences p72
Experiences p76
Eating p80
Drinking p81
Shopping p81
MINAMI-AZABU
Kurayami-zaka

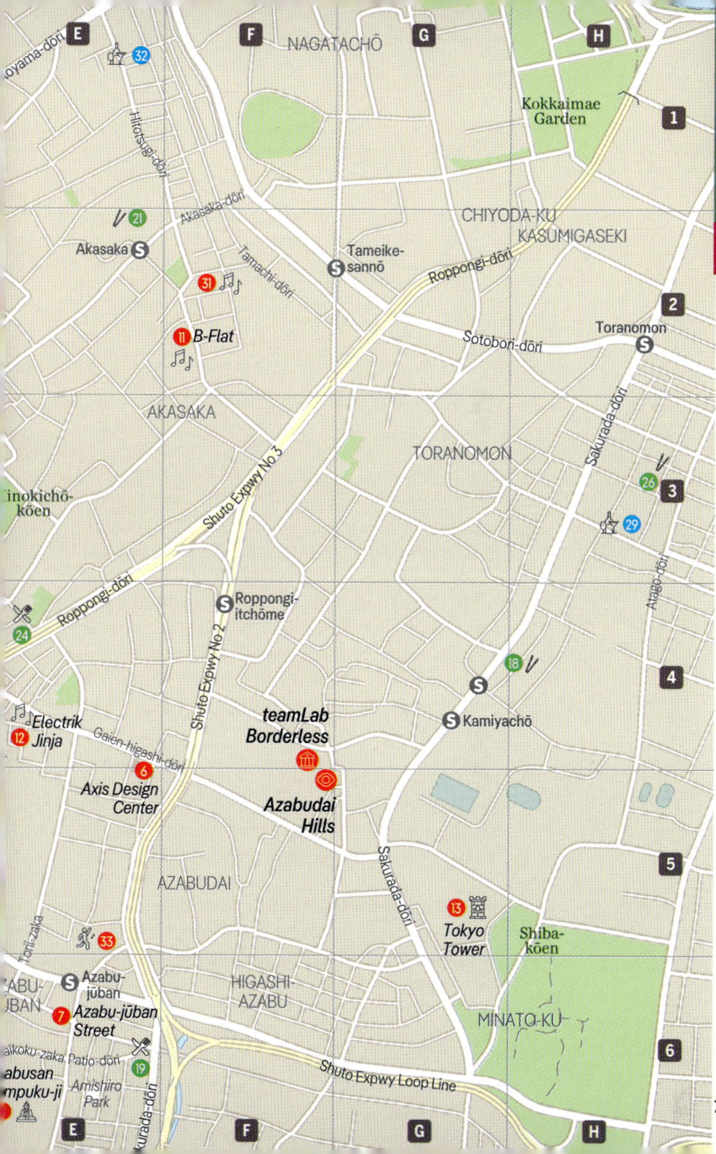

E
F
NAGATACHŌ
G
H
32
1
Kokkaimae
Garden
Hitotsugi-dōri
Akasaka-dōri
21
CHIYODA-KU
KASUMIGASEKI
Akasaka
Tameike-
sannō
Roppongi-dōri
31
2
Toranomon
Tamachi-dōri
11 B-Flat
Sotobori-dōri
Sakurada-dōri
AKASAKA
TORANOMON
26
3
29
inokichō-
kōen
Shuto Expwy No 3
Atago-dōri
Roppongi-dōri
Roppongi-
itchōme
18
24
4
Kamiyachō
Electrik
Jinja
12
teamLab
Borderless
Shuto Expwy No 2
Gaien-higashi-dōri
6
Axis Design
Center
Azabudai
Hills
5
AZABUDAI
Sakurada-dōri
13
Tokyo
Tower
Shiba-
kōen
Torii-zaka
33
MINATO-KU
Azabu-
jūban
HIGASHI-
AZABU
ABU-
JŪBAN
7 Azabu-jūban
Street
Daikoku-zaka
Patio-dōri
aikoku-zaka
19
abusan
mpuku-ji
Amishiro
Park
Kurada-dōri
Shuto Expwy Loop Line
6
E
F
G
H

teamLab Borderless

Tokyo's newest big development, Azabudai Hills, is the home of teamLab Borderless: MORI Building DIGITAL ART MUSEUM *(adult/child approx ¥3600/2800)*, the responsive digital art museum that that has emerged as one of Tokyo's top attractions. The newest 'Hills' is also an attraction in its own right.

MAP P70 **F4**

PLANNING TIP
Purchase teamLab Borderless tickets online in advance, as they may sell out. The museum is open 8am to 9pm and closes once a month. Check the website for details.

Scan this QR code for teamLab Borderless opening times and tickets.

Digital Art at teamLab Borderless

Art collective teamLab formed in Tokyo in the 2000s and has since become a big name in digital art – a medium that uses digital technology, including augmented reality, to dazzling effect.

While you can now see their works at other global hot spots, teamLab Borderless remains the collective's signature experience, home to more than 50 hypnotic artworks. The installations feel like discrete worlds, which you can explore at leisure, pausing to interact with digital avatars, which may respond to your presence or even beckon you to play. Download the teamlab app to unlock more ways to engage with the installations.

Sketch Ocean is one of the most popular attractions. Visitors design a fish – on paper – which then appears as a digital image in the ocean artwork. At Sketch Factory, you can order merchandise such as T-shirts and totes printed with your drawings.

Exploring Azabudai Hills

Future-forward **Azabudai Hills** (MAP P70 **F5**) has trippy, sinuous architecture, garden terraces and public artworks, such as Miss Forest in its central green space. Most attractions are in the Garden Plaza buildings, including teamLab Borderless.

Roppongi Hills

The star attraction at Roppongi Hills is the Mori Art Museum, a popular centre for contemporary art. It shares the top floors of Mori Tower with an observatory, Tokyo City View. Other reasons to visit include the cinema and huge selection of eateries.

MAP P70 **D5**

Mori Art Museum & Tokyo City View

The **Mori Art Museum** (MAM; *adult/child from ¥2000/1700*) is Tokyo's largest space for contemporary art, staging several blockbuster shows each year. These have included retrospectives of prominent Japanese artists, such as Takashi Murakami, Yayoi Kusama and Makoto Aida; there have also been thought-provoking exhibitions on AI, urbanism and climate change. Every three years, the museum puts on Roppongi Crossing, an exhibition of up-and-coming artists *(next in 2028)*.

MAM also has three smaller spaces (including one for film) spotlighting more experimental work. Admission includes entry to **Tokyo City View**, which has vistas from 250m; it's especially good for spotting Tokyo Tower.

PLANNING TIP
The Mori Art Museum and Tokyo City View are open until 10pm (except Tuesdays), later than many other museums. Most Roppongi Hills restaurants are open until 11pm.

Hanging Out at Roppongi Hills

The other big attraction is the state-of-the-art movie theatre, **Toho Cinemas Roppongi Hills** (*toho theater.jp; adult/child from ¥2000/1000*). Movies are screened past midnight, and you can order wine and beer. Elsewhere in the mall, there are multiple food halls with options ranging from fast food to Michelin-starred. All of this makes Roppongi Hills a popular destination for that classic night out – dinner and a movie.

Scan this QR code to book tickets for the Mori Art Museum.

Walk Roppongi

While you can access major attractions directly via underground subway passages, this walk gives you a sense of direction at street level, starting with the neighbourhood's signature intersection, Roppongi Crossing. From there, weave through Roppongi Hills in the direction of Azabu-jūban, a charming district that offers a contrast to all the development in Roppongi.

START	END	LENGTH
Roppongi Crossing	Azabu-jūban	2km; 1½hr

1 The Main Intersection

Take Exit 3 from Roppongi's subway station, which puts you on the corner of **Roppongi Crossing**. Here you'll find **Almond**, a long-running cake shop and local landmark. While it's usually quiet during the day, after dark this street corner fills with friends meeting up for an evening out.

2 Art Galleries

On your way to Roppongi Hills, take a detour down the side street on your left for **Complex 665** (p76), a grey non-descript building that houses three influential contemporary art galleries – perfect for taking the pulse of the local scene (and free, too!).

3 A Famous Public Sculpture

Roppongi's most famous work of art, however, remains Maman, one of several public sculptures at **Roppongi Hills** (p73). The giant spider, by Louise Bourgeois, has an amusing way of messing with the scale of the buildings, especially in photos. It's also a useful landmark for navigating the mall; keep walking and you'll pass the entrance to the Mori Art Museum and Toho Cinemas Roppongi Hills.

4 A Pretty Street

Opposite the mall is **Keiyaki-zaka**, dotted with art sculptures and trees. In spring, it's lined with cherry blossoms; in winter, bare branches are bright with fairy lights. It's a popular date spot and often appears in TV shows. **Bricolage Bread & Co.** (p80), one of Tokyo's rare alfresco eating options, is at the top of the street.

5 An Iconic Shopping Street

At the bottom of Keiyaki-zaka, round the corner towards Azabu-jūban. To avoid the main road, take the side street on the right, which leads to the next attraction: **Azabu-jūban Street** (p77), a historic market street with venerable old shops alongside trendy new ones.

6 A Famous Sweets Stop

On an alleyway on the left, look out for **Naniwaya Sōhonten**, a local favourite for *taiyaki* (fish-shaped bean cakes) since 1909. Consider yourself lucky if you can actually score one of these traditional treats, as they're known to sell out fast. From here, it's a short walk to the Azabu-jūban subway station, or you can continue exploring the neighbourhood.

EXPERIENCES

Surround Yourself with Design in Tokyo Midtown
SHOPPING & DESIGN

Tokyo Midtown (MAP: **1** P70 **D3**) sets itself apart with its emphasis on design. As well as shops galore in its mall, Galleria, the complex is home to two notable Tokyo galleries: **21_21 Design Sight** (MAP: **2** P70 **D3**; *2121designsight.jp; adult/child ¥1600/free*) and the **Suntory Museum of Art** (MAP: **3** P70 **D3**; *suntory.com/sma; adult/ child ¥1800/free*).

Galleria is the place to visit if you enjoy shops focused on Japanese craftsmanship. Shops include Hida, a classic Japanese woodworking company; Style Meets People, selling homeware and ceramics by independent designers; and the Cover Nippon, which stocks a mind-boggling amount of trinkets from across Japan. On the same floor is the Suntory Museum of Art, in a space designed by famous architect Kengo Kuma. It features exhibitions showcasing objects of beauty with purpose, such as tea ceremony ceramics.

Across from Galleria is 21_21 Design Sight, housed in an elegant, concrete-and-glass structure by Tadao Ando, another of Japan's preeminent contemporary architects. It hosts changing exhibitions that explore how we interact with design in daily life through the products we use and the spaces we inhabit.

Gallery-Hop at Complex 665
ART & DESIGN

Thanks to the pull of major institutions like the Mori Art Museum and 21_21 Design Sight, Roppongi has become one of Tokyo's best spots for gallery hopping. **Complex 665** (MAP: **4** P70 **D4**) is a good place to start: the small building houses three influential galleries – Taka Ishii (*taka ishiigallery.com; free)*, ShugoArts (*shugoarts.com; free)* and Tomio Koyama Gallery (*tomiokoyama gallery.com; free)* – that represent contemporary artists working both in Japan and abroad.

Want to see more? There are several more small galleries in **Piramide** (MAP: **5** P70 **D4**), a mall-type space near Complex 665. Taka Ishii also has another space, **Taka Ishii Gallery Photography / Film**, in the **Axis Design Center** (MAP: **6** P70 **E5**; *center.axisinc.co.jp; free)* on Higashi-Gaien-dōri.

The galleries are all free to enter and you can check ahead to see what's on – Tokyo Art Beat (*tokyoart beat.com)* is a great resource – or just turn up for something unexpected. Most are open from around noon to 6pm or 7pm and closed on Sundays, Mondays, national holidays and between exhibitions.

Explore the Cobblestone Streets of Azabu-jūban
NEIGHBOURHOOD

Azabu-jūban is a prestigious residential district, home to foreign embassies, old-money estates and celebrity penthouses. It also has a charming village-like feel, thanks to its cobblestone streets, low-rise development and local protectionism. The few chain shops that can be found here famously have discreet signage to blend in with the atmosphere – just like parts of Kyoto. Anime fans, meanwhile, might know Azabu-jūban as the main setting for the *Sailor Moon* manga/anime franchise.

For visitors, the main attraction is historic **Azabu-jūban Street** (MAP: **7** P70 **E6**), a market throughfare with 300 years of history. Follow other narrow, winding streets to discover more local shops and restaurants, as well as neighbourhood shrines and temples. **Azabusan Zempuku-ji** (MAP: **8** P70 **E6**; *azabu-san.or.jp; free*), Tokyo's second-oldest temple – after Asakusa's **Sensō-ji** – can be found here; it's home to an ancient ginkgo tree, said to be Tokyo's oldest.

As you explore, just remember to keep your voices down, as this is still largely a residential neighbourhood.

See Roppongi after Dark
NIGHTLIFE

Roppongi is famous for nightlife and, despite recent redevelopment, you'll still find plenty of party spots around Roppongi Crossing, as well as down Gaien-Higashi-dōri. Options include shot bars, sports bars, clubs and karaoke parlours – most of which stay open past dawn. Whether you're into hip-hop

GLORIOUS GARDENS
If you fancy a break from the Roppongi skyscrapers, the **Midtown Garden** (MAP: **9** P70 **D3**; *en.tokyo-midtown.com; free*) is one of the easiest ways to step out and breathe green.

The landscape design incorporates elements found in traditional Japanese gardens. Across four zones, the design moves fluidly between stones, a pond and garden-specific plants, fostering a sense of harmony within the space. There are 400 trees, including 140 inherited from the site's previous occupants, grounding the area with large trees including cherry blossom and camphor. The garden runs a programme of events through the year, including *hanami* (blossom viewing) in the spring and illuminations during winter.

parties, underground techno or VIP rooms, Roppongi caters to many tastes. There are plenty of late-night eating options, too.

For music lovers, a trip to see live bands at **Blue Note Tokyo** (MAP: **10** P70 **A5**) in nearby Aoyama or **B-Flat** (MAP: **11** P70 **F2**) in Akasaka should be followed by a music bar crawl around Roppongi. The area is home to countless bars and speakeasies serving drinks with a side of live music, and many are frequented by players looking for some downtime after their big shows. One such spot is **Electrik Jinja** (MAP: 12 P70 **E4**; *instagram.com/electrik_jinja; entry price varies*), a basement bar with a band set-up that sees musicians jamming most nights.

Spot Tokyo Tower from the Street

LANDMARK

Completed in 1958, **Tokyo Tower** (MAP: 13 P70 **G5**; *tokyotower.co.jp; adult/child from ¥1800/¥1000*) is a beloved symbol of the capital – even if it's no longer Tokyo's tallest structure (that's **Tokyo Skytree**). At 333m tall, it's just slightly taller than the Eiffel Tower, which it resembles in form but not in colour: Tokyo Tower is a can't-miss-it shade of red (technically 'international orange', as required by aviation law).

There are observatories open to the public for a fee; however, better than the view *from* Tokyo Tower is the view *of* Tokyo Tower. While it once presided over central Tokyo, decades of development have made spotting the famous landmark something of an elusive (but rewarding) sport – like catching sight of Mt Fuji emerging from the clouds. Roppongi provides good angles, especially from Gaien-Higashi-dōri (east of Roppongi Crossing).

Tokyo Tower is illuminated every night, from dusk to midnight, in warm tones for winter and cool tones for summer, plus a special colour display on Mondays.

Sample Japanese Sweets at Toraya

GOURMET

Founded 500 years ago in Kyoto, Toraya is one of Japan's most famous traditional confectioners and a great introduction to *wagashi* (Japanese sweets). The main Tokyo-based store, **Toraya Akasaka** (MAP: 14 P70 **D1**; *global.toraya-group.co.jp*), is a bona-fide *wagashi* destination set across three floors. Its basement gallery hosts free *wagashi*-themed exhibitions; its top-floor tea salon serves dessert sets with freshly made sweets and tea or coffee; and, of course, its shop sells sweets to take home.

REDESIGNING ROPPONGI

Roppongi's reputation for raucous nightlife dates to the US occupation of Japan after WWII, when America had a large local presence (there's still a recreational barracks nearby). Roppongi Hills, which opened in 2003, heralded a shift. These complexes – which now include Toranomon Hills and Azabudai Hills – are the life's work of the late real estate tycoon Minoru Mori, who had a singular vision for a new kind of 'modern urban village' that would combine office space, residences and amenities in dense, designer packages. They impress some and leave others cold; visit and see for yourself.

The tea salon is worth the likely wait: try the house speciality, *yō-kan,* a dense bean jelly considered the ultimate traditional Japanese sweet; or the seasonal fresh sweets, called *namagashi,* styled in shapes and colours that – like much of classical Japanese art – reflect the changing seasons.

Traditional Japanese sweets are made with few ingredients – often a combination of adzuki beans, sugar and agar-agar; so they're often vegan, but check to be sure. The cafe and shop close at 5.30pm and 6pm respectively, but for a later experience visit the smaller **Toraya Tokyo Midtown** (MAP: 15 P70 **D3**; *until 9pm*).

Hang Out at the National Art Center
ART & DESIGN

The **National Art Center Tokyo** (NACT; MAP: 16 P70 **C4**; *nact.jp; adult/ child approx ¥2000/free*) contains the country's largest exhibition space for visiting shows, usually from prestigious international institutions like the Musée de Cluny in Paris or Vienna's Kunsthistorisches Museum. It also curates its own shows, often on contemporary Japanese art.

No matter what's on, the building itself is spectacular, with an awesome undulating glass facade designed by influential architect Kishō Kurokawa. It's free to enter; you only have to pay for admission to the galleries. Take advantage of the bright, airy space and have a coffee at one of the museum's two cafes, casual **Café**

Consider visiting when one of these popular festivals takes over Roppongi venues – and streets.

Roppongi Art Night
Annual event with visually spectacular installations and street performances around Roppongi Hills. Held over two days (and one night) in spring or autumn, depending on the year.

Art Week Tokyo
Many of Roppongi's major institutions are on the organising committee for this contemporary art event, which sees over 50 local galleries link up each November.

Design Touch
Tokyo Midtown's annual autumn design festival sees cool installations take over Midtown Garden, plus exhibitions and pop-up shops for interior goods around the mall.

Coquille in the atrium lobby or the fancier **Salon de Thé Rond**, perched on an inverted glass cone.

NACT is open daily from 10am to 6pm, except Tuesdays. While you're here, head to the basement to check out the excellent gift shop, **Souvenir from Tokyo** (MAP: 17 P70 **C3**), where you can find an ever-changing selection of covetable gifts by local designers.

Best Places for...

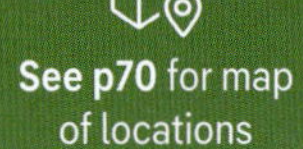

Ⓨ Budget　**ⓎⓎ** Midrange　**ⓎⓎⓎ** Top End

Eating

Japanese Home Comforts

Echigoya Genpaku Sohonzan Ⓨ

 **18** H4

A local lunchtime favourite: perfectly cooked grilled fish, along with the standard sides of rice, miso soup and pickles. *echigoya-genpaku-souhonzan.com; 11am-4pm & 6-11pm Mon-Fri, 11am-2.30pm Sat*

Itohan ⓎⓎ

19 E6

Beloved spot that has served the people of Azabu their *monja-yaki*—Tokyo's take on Osaka's savoury pancake, *okono-miyaki* — for decades. *noon-3pm (last order 2.30pm), 6-10pm Wed-Sun*

Ramen, Soba & Udon

Lilyan ⓎⓎ

 **20** D4

Loved by locals and travellers alike, Lilyan serves soba (buckwheat) noodles cooked in its open kitchen, alongside a selection of natural wines and *nihonshū* (sake). *lilyan.jp; 11.30am-2.30pm & 6-11pm*

Ramen Mozu Ⓨ

 **21** E2

Mozu serves up an impressive variety of ramen, with *shio, shōyu* and vegetarian *shio* broth options, with toppings such as *wagyū, menma* and crispy fried shallots. *ramenmozu.group; 11am-11pm*

TsuruTonTan Ⓨ

22 D4

Huge, steaming bowls of udon (thick wheat noodles) in classic and novel styles (such as 'udon carbonara'), ideal for carb-loading after a night out. *tsurutontan. co.jp; 11am-8am*

Lunchtime Hot Spots

Bricolage Bread & Co. Ⓨ

 **23** C5

Be prepared to queue for this delicious French bread, born from its founder's experience after the 2011 earthquake. *bricolagebread.com; 9am-7.30pm Tue-Sun*

Common ⓎⓎ

 **24** E4

Uber-cool spot Common serves coffee, brunch and dinner daily, with lounge DJs Thursdays to Saturdays. Its walls host changing exhibitions by contemporary local artists. *instagram.com/ common_tokyo; 8am-11pm*

Lively Dinnertime Hangouts

Gonpachi ⓎⓎ

 **25** B5

The restaurant that inspired a memorable scene in Quentin Tarantino's *Kill Bill* (2003) serves charcoal skewers, sashimi platters and other *izakaya* staples. *gonpachi.jp/nishi -azabu; 11.30am-3am*

Toranomon Yokochō ⓎⓎ

 **26** H3

A food court with oulets of 26 exceptional establishments. Their main restaurants may have Michelin stars and impossible-to-reserve seats, but here you can enjoy their offerings in an informal setting. *toranomonhills.com/ toranomonyokocho; 11am-11pm*

Drinking

Coffee and Matcha

Wasachi
27 D4

Get your matcha fix down an unassuming side street. Choose strong to weak and different types of milk. *instagram.com/ wasachi_japan; 9.30am- 5pm Mon-Fri*

Tapirosu
28 D5

Enjoy serious, old-school coffee at Tapirosu, run by a charming Japanese man who brews his own beans. European- baroque-style interior. *tapirosu.blog.fc2.com; 11am-9pm Mon-Tue & Thu- Fri; from noon Sat & Sun*

Cocktails & Mocktails

Rooftop Bar at Andaz Tokyo
29 H3

Get that luxury hotel experience by admiring sky-high views while sipping delectable cocktails at Tokyo's highest rooftop bar. *restaurants.andaztokyo .jp/en/rooftop-bar; 5pm-midnight Sun-Thu, to 1am Fri-Sat*

These
30 B5

Step into These's book-lined interior, choose a cocktail from the fruit basket and while the night away whispering, reading and sipping. *these-jp.com; 6pm-3am Mon-Sat, to 2am Sun*

Music Bars

G's Bar
31 E1

Bob along to live jazz from pros every night 8pm till 10.30pm at this friendly basement spot. Hang around afterwards for lively banter. *g-s-bar. com; 7pm-2am Mon-Sat*

Bar Luther
32 E1

Drink whisky and gin while the bartender mixes old soul, rock and blues all night long at this popular analoguw hide-away. *luther-yokohama .jp/mellow-groove; 7pm-3.30am Mon-Sat*

Clubs & Lounges

1Oak Tokyo
33 F2

A favourite with visiting celebs, 1Oak – which also has clubs in LA, Dubai and Shanghai – is a fashionable place to dance to (mostly) hip-hop. *1oaktokyo.com; 11pm-5am, from 10pm Fri & Sat*

Shisha Bar Rakuen
34 E5

See your shisha smoke create patterns with strategically positioned laser artistry. High-quality tobacco, cocktails and playlists. *rakuen-one. com; 8pm-5am*

Shopping

Art & Design

Mori Art Museum Shop
35 D5

Limited-edition artist collaborations in the museum shop, plus art books and more. Check out its bigger branch in Roppongi Hills' West Walk (3rd floor; no museum ticket required). *art-view.roppongihills .com/en/shop; 11am-9pm*

The Cover Nippon
36 D3

Small but curated collection of goods from Japanese brands: one of several design-oriented shops in the Galleria at Tokyo Midtown. *thecover nippon.jp; 11am-8pm*

See p98
for eating
and shopping
listings

Explore
Shibuya & Ebisu

Researched by
Cherise Fong

Thanks to its iconic intersection, Shibuya (澁谷) could be a visual shorthand for Tokyo in the global imagination: pulsating with energy, in perpetual transformation. A pilgrimage site for young people throughout Japan that draws trendsetters from around the globe, this once-suburban district has rapidly developed into a dynamic centre for progressive youth culture and innovation – particularly in design, tech startups, fashion and performing arts. Ebisu (恵比寿), named after the pioneering brand of beer, is another lively, if more understated, district with notable drinking holes. The neighbouring upscale residential enclaves of Daikanyama and Naka-Meguro, along with up-and-coming Shimo-Kitazawa, are stylishly low-rise and low-key.

Getting Around

 **Walking**

Given the density of people, shops and all-around stimulation in Shibuya and Ebisu, these districts are best explored on foot. The quieter surrounding neighbourhoods are also pleasantly walkable, from Daikanyama's short but steep hills to the Meguro riverside.

 **Train**

Shibuya Station is a major hub, with train lines segueing into subway lines and vice-versa. Shibuya and Ebisu are adjacent on the circular Yamanote Line and Shimo-Kitazawa is just one rapid-express stop away. The Ginza line connects Shibuya directly to Asakusa.

THE BEST

ICONIC EXPERIENCE
Scramble Crossing (p85)

LOCAL BREWERY
Yebisu Brewery
Tokyo (p88)

VIEWPOINT
Shibuya Sky (p87)

THRIFT SHOPPING
Shimo-Kitazawa (p96)

BAR-HOPPING
Ebisu (p96)

Shibuya Scramble Crossing (p85)

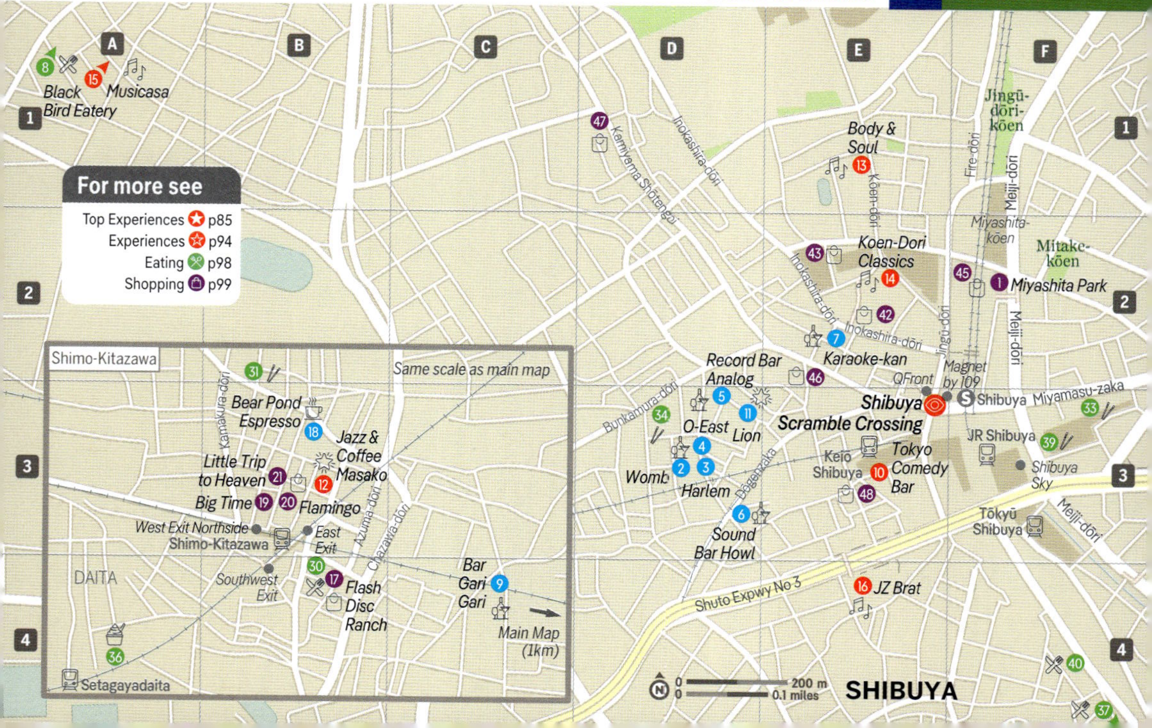

SHIBUYA

Jingū-dōri-kōen

Fire-dōri

Meiji-dōri

Mitake-kōen

Miyashita-kōen

1 Miyashita Park

Meiji-dōri

Jingū-dōri

45

Magnet by 109

QFront

Shibuya Miyamasu-zaka

33

39

Shibuya Sky

JR Shibuya

Tōkyū Shibuya

Meiji-dōri

40

37

Body & Soul

13 Kōen-dōri

Koen-Dōri Classics

14

42

Inokashira-dōri

7

43

Inokashira-dōri

46

Karaoke-kan

S Shibuya

Scramble Crossing

Tokyo Comedy Bar

10

Keiō Shibuya

48

16 JZ Brat

Inokashira-dōri

Kamiyama Shōtengai

47

Record Bar Analog

5

11

O-East Lion

4

3

Harlem

6

Sound Bar Howl

2

Womb

34

Bunkamura-dōri

Dōgenzaka

Shuto Expwy No 3

200 m

0.1 miles

0

0

N

For more see

Top Experiences p85

Experiences p94

Eating p98

Shopping p99

Black Musicasa Bird Eatery

15

8

A

Same scale as main map

Shimo-Kitazawa

Bar Gari Gari

9

Main Map (1km)

Azuma-dōri

Chazawa-dōri

Jazz & Coffee Masako

Bear Pond Espresso

18

12

Little Trip to Heaven

21

Flamingo

20

East Exit

Flash

17

Disc Ranch

30

Big Time

19

Kamakura-dōri

West Exit Northside Shimo-Kitazawa

Southwest Exit

31

DAITA

36

Setagayadaita

Shibuya Scramble Crossing

One of Tokyo's most iconic sights is a sprawling intersection where pedestrians scramble across from multiple directions. It's a mesmerising sight, especially when viewed from above. Several hundred people on average cross at once, from selfie-shooting tourists to weekend shoppers to anyone who wants to join in the fray.

MAP: P84 **E3**

Dive into the Intersection

If the Crossing looks familiar, maybe that's because it has appeared in countless films, such as *Your Name*. Situated at the Hachikō exit of the labyrinthine Shibuya Station, the **Scramble Crossing** is a starburst nexus of people flowing in all directions with both apparent chaos and balletic precision. Enter at ground level, get caught up in the swarm and feel the rush of pure adrenaline that is scrambling to the other side.

Scramble for Views

The Crossing can be viewed from various heights above street level. Inside **Shibuya Station**, look for (free) views of the intersection from the elevated passage across from the Myth of Tomorrow mural. For a more immersive view closer to the action, Magnet mall's 2nd-floor **Hoshino Coffee** offers front-row mezzanine seats from its long wooden counter. Across the street at **QFront**, take the escalators past Starbucks up to the **Share Lounge** on the 3rd and stealthy 4th floors for a much more intimate window seat. Back at **Magnet by 109**, head straight up to the 7th floor for late-night views with drinks and DJs, or to the dedicated 8th-floor open-air roof deck (*¥1800, includes one drink*).

PLANNING TIP
While the Scramble is best experienced from the ground up, be sure not to linger in the street, as the green light gives pedestrians only just enough time to cross.

Scan this QR code for more info on visiting Shibuya Sky.

EBISU
DAIKANYAMA
SARUGAKU-CHŌ
Kyū-Yamate-dōri
Hachiman-dōri
HIRO-O
For more see
Top Experiences p85
Experiences p94
Eating p98
Shopping p99
Log Road Daikanyama
26
T-Site
27 28 Tsutaya Books
49
AOBADAI
Meguro-gawa
Yamate-dōri
Kyū-Yamate-dōri
Daikanyama
35
EBISU NISHI
41
24
Janai Coffee
38
Meiji-dōri
Komazawa-dōri
Ebisu-higashi kōen
32
Meiji-dōri
Ebisu
Ebisu-yokochō
EBISU
Shibuya-gawa
Sato Sakura Museum
29
44
Ebisu-kōen
25
AlO
Komazawa-dōri
Ebisu
Bar Martha
22
Naka-Meguro
Naka-Meguro
Komazawa-dōri
NAKA-MEGURO
KAMI-MEGURO
Bar Track
23
EBISU-MINAMI
Ebisu-minami kōen
Sky Walk
Yebisu Bar Stand
Blue Sea
Blue Note Place
Yebisu Brewery Tokyo
Kusunoki-dōri
Galen-nishi-dōri
Yebisu Garden Place
Platanus-dōri
TOP Museum
MITA
Jakuzure-isewaki-dōri
Chaya-zaka (Slope)
MEGURO-KU
Shuto Expwy No 2
Tokyo Metropolitan Teien Art Museum
Shirokanedai
Institute for Nature Study
Comodo
KAMI-ŌSAKI
SHINAGAWA-KU
N
0 500 m
0 0.25 miles

AIMUSE/SHUTTERSTOCK

Shibuya Sky

The 46th-floor rooftop that crowns Shibuya's tallest building, **Scramble Square**, overlooks the Scramble Crossing, the entire neighbourhood and beyond to the horizon, giving context to the crowds on the scale of a city. **Shibuya Sky** (pictured above; *adult/child from ¥2700/1200*) has an indoor lounge that's pleasantly bright and temperature-controlled, but the open-air roof deck is the highlight. The transparent barriers all but disappear in photos and hammocks are built right into the deck. Tickets are time-slotted for entry to avoid overcrowding, but there is no time limit for enjoying the views.

QUICK BREAK
Head to the basement levels of Scramble Square for various sweet treats, as well as *bentō* and sushi sets, which you can eat at the counter area in the centre.

Yebisu Garden Place

This classically styled plaza was inaugurated in 1994 on the site of the original Yebisu beer brewery, with a revived taproom. It's also home to a serious photography museum, a red-brick jazz club, an art-house cinema and a 40-storey office tower with fine dining at the top.

MAP P86 **D3**

PLANNING TIP
For more Yebisu beer (and food) after taproom hours, head over to Yebisu Bar Stand at the top of the plaza, open till 10pm.

Scan this QR code for sites and events at Yebisu Garden Place.

Taste Yebisu from the Tap

Yebisu, now a popular premium label under Suntory, is one of Japan's oldest beers. It was first brewed here in a red-brick factory in the 1890s, giving the neighbourhood its name: Ebisu is a modern spelling of Yebisu. While the original factory closed in the 1980s (making way for **Yebisu Garden Place**), beer-making returned to Ebisu in 2024 with the opening of **Yebisu Brewery Tokyo**. The craft-sized facility produces Yebisu Infinity, a new 'prototype' beer for the label, which you can try alongside other Yebisu limited-edition and seasonal brews at the in-house taproom. The free museum area retraces the history of the brand through vintage bottles, photographs, posters and other original artefacts, including Yebisu's striking wooden signboards from the 1920s.

Browse a TOP Museum Gallery

The **Tokyo Photographic Art Museum** (TOP Museum; *exhibition prices vary*) is undeniably a photographer's museum, with featured exhibitions often curated by photographers' associations. The three gallery spaces are each charged separately, making it easy to drop in for an exhibit – a retrospective of a major artist, a selection of

COWARDLION/SHUTTERSTOCK

documentary photos from the archives or themed shows from the collection. If you're feeling peckish, the ground-floor Komagura cafe serves homemade vegetable curry.

Experience the Central Plaza

A big part of Ebisu's chic image is the large covered plaza surrounded by a faux-marbled shopping arcade at the centre of Yebisu Garden Place. Most weekends, it hosts events and attractions for local residents: an organic farmers market, live music, outdoor movie screenings in summer, Baccarat crystal illuminations in winter, a Christmas market, etc. On certain nights, you can even hear the live jazz playing through **Blue Note Place**'s open terrace.

QUICK BREAK
At the top of the plaza, the Okinawan ice-cream brand Blue Seal specialises in tropical island flavours, such as sugar cane or shiikwāsā sherbet.

Teien Art Museum

Although the Tokyo Metropolitan Teien Art Museum (*exhibition prices vary*) often hosts compelling exhibitions of decorative arts, its chief appeal lies in the building itself. It's an authentic Art Deco structure and former princely estate built in 1933, designed by leading French Art Deco figures, with much of the original interior intact.

MAP P86 **E4**

PLANNING TIP

Save extra time to leisurely stroll through the gardens and lounge on the lawn space. The Institute for Nature Study has a separate entrance and closes earlier.

Scan this QR code to see what's on at the Teien Art Museum

Visit the Manor

It was during the golden age of Art Deco that Prince Asaka Yasuhiko and Princess Nobuko stayed in France and they wasted no time in commissioning the style's top designers, including Henri Rapin and René Lalique, to decorate their new residence in Tokyo. Even a century later, every room is a well-preserved wonder of the style, showcasing fine wooden frameworks and furniture, glass relief doors and chandeliers, stained and etched glass panels, wood inlay floorings, iron finishings on staircases and radiators. And with more than 20 types of stone in various colours and patterns, the entire building is like a sample book of domestically quarried materials. Witness the French Vert d'Estours green marble bathrooms.

Wander the Garden

It's no coincidence that the museum is named after its gardens, with a rich diversity of flora, where something is in bloom at almost any time of year. The lawn space and Japanese Garden, built around a koi pond, have been preserved since the Prince Asaka family lived here. The original Kouka Teahouse, completed by a master *sukiya* carpenter in 1936, also includes a rare Western-style room

CAITO/SHUTTERSTOCK

to accommodate foreign guests. The more recently converted European Garden is full of cherry blossoms in spring.

Walk Through Wild Nature

Surrounding the gardens, the rare natural forest of what is now the **Institute for Nature Study** *(ins. kahaku.go.jp; adult/child ¥320/free)* was once the secondary home of a feudal lord. Later the manor on the grounds was used as a military storehouse, before becoming an imperial estate in the Taishō period (1912–1925). During all this time, the landlords pretty much let the local flora go wild. Since 1949, the area has been open to the public as a Natural Monument and Historic Site, home to some 500 native plant species.

TAKE A BREAK
Next to Teien Garden's main gate, the very fancy Comodo restaurant serves French-Italian fusion cuisine for both lunch and dinner, and stays open after the museum closes.

Walk Ebisu

The Tokyo Toilet Project commissioned 16 top architects to design public toilets around Shibuya Ward, in an effort to combine functionality, accessibility, cleanliness and safety, all with a dash of style. This walk takes you past four of these designer restrooms, all permanently ensconced in Ebisu's glowing nightlife district.

START	END	LENGTH
Ebisu Park	Japanese Ice Ouca	1.2km; ½hr

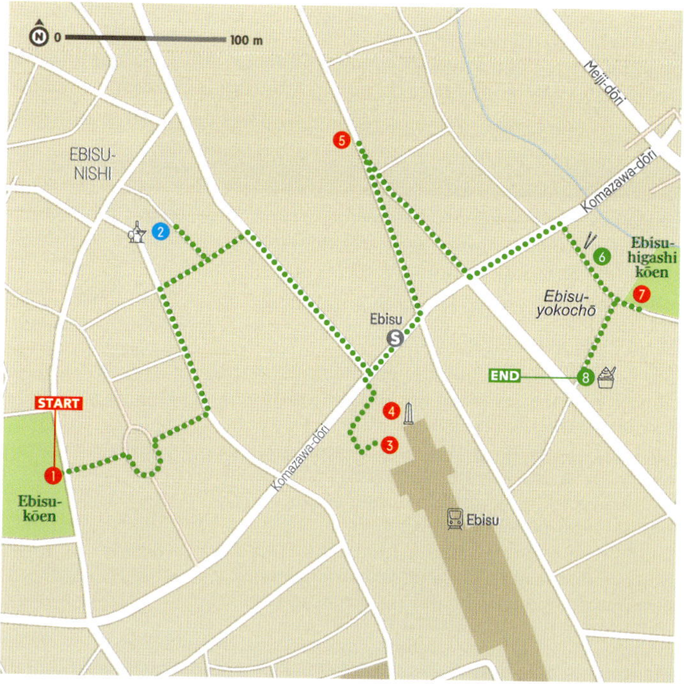

1 Stone Age Toilet

Start on the west side of **Ebisu Park**. The lightly textured concrete toilet designed by Masamichi Katayama (Wonderwall) is a nod to prehistoric Japan's primitive river huts, often made of hardened soil or pieces of wood bound together.

2 Bar Trench

Cross the street and continue past the tiny Ebisu Shrine for a quick prayer, then up a street lined with bars and restaurants. Around the corner, **Bar Trench**, a pioneer of Tokyo's vibrant cocktail scene, emits old-world bohemianism with a perfectly chilled playlist and original cocktails crafted with absinthe, botanical infusions and bitters.

3 Cube Toilet

Head down to **Ebisu Station**'s West Exit, where you'll find the inconspicuously glowing white jewel-box toilet designed by Kashiwa Satō.

4 Jolly Deity

Right beside it, the mounted bronze **Ebisu Statue** by Shigeru Kinoshita depicts the smiling, portly god of fortune and divine patron of fishermen holding a fat sea bream, symbol of prosperity.

5 Vermilion Toilet

Walk under the train tracks then left up the street and around the corner. Nao Tamura's triangular red **Higashi Sanchōme** toilet was inspired by *origata,* a traditional Japanese method of decorative wrapping, in the spirit of hospitality.

6 Tasty Alley

Head down to cross the main street, turn left then right. On the right of the street, **Ebisu-yokochō** is chock-a-block with *izakaya* (Japanese pub-eateries) dishing up everything from classic street food to sumptuous grilled seafood and is animated every night of the week. **Afuri** (p98), serving its signature yuzu salt ramen, is also across the street and open till 5am.

7 Squid Toilet

A few steps further inside **Ebisu East Park** (Ebisu-higashi kōen) with its signature Octopus Slide is Fumihiko Maki's white Squid Toilet, featuring a playfully sloped pavilion roof and even a bench to sit down and rest with a view of the playground.

8 Ice Cream

Walk down the side street to **Japanese Ice Ouca** for a triple-scoop dessert: creamy refined ice cream in typical Japanese flavours – sweet milk, black sesame, *kokutō* (brown sugar), *karintō* (deep-fried dough) or *kinako* (soy-bean powder), served with roasted green tea and salty seaweed.

EXPERIENCES

Hang Out at Miyashita Park

SHOPPING

MAP: **1** P84 **F2**

Formerly a railroad track, **Miyashita Park** *(miyashita-park.tokyo)* is now a low-rise semi-open-air mall whose various shops epitomise Shibuya's reputation for trendsetting youth culture. There's even one shop dedicated to Shibuya/Hachikō-themed souvenirs, as well as an open dance studio, food court, tapas bars and the always lively Shibuya-yokochō at ground level, which serves regional specialities from across Japan.

But the best part of the mall is its generous rooftop – a public park and recreational green space that stretches from a skatepark and beach volleyball courts to a Starbucks stand to a high-rise hotel that offers splendid views over the park and beyond. There are plenty of benches, both on the rooftop itself and on the east-facing outdoor terraces, where you can just sit down with a drink and look out over the surrounding neighbourhood, while feeling like you're right in the heart of it.

Have a Night Out in Dōgenzaka

NIGHTLIFE

In Tokyo, hills are more likely to have names than streets and Dōgenzaka is one of them. Shibuya's most famous nightclub is here, the warehouse-style **Womb** (MAP: **2** P84 **D3**; *womb.co.jp*), specialising in techno and house. **Harlem** (MAP: **3** P84 **D3**; *harlem.co.jp*) focuses on hip-hop, while **O-East** (MAP: **4** P84 **D3**; *shibuya-o.com/east*) spotlights Japanese bands – and includes the sleek, artsy DJ Bar Azumaya *(azumaya. jp)*, which serves sake and Japanese spice-accented cocktails.

The cult **Record Bar Analog** (MAP: **5** P84 **D3**; *analog-recordbar. com*) welcomes you to chill out on sofas, where you can request one song from their retro vinyl collection. Or relax with a fancy drink at **Sound Bar Howl** (MAP: **6** P84 **D3**; *wam-inc.jp/howl*), which projects golden-age Hollywood movies on the wall and pop music on the speakers. The bar closes at 4.30am, just in time for you to catch the sunrise.

Sing Your Heart Out at Karaoke

POP CULTURE

MAP: **7** P84 **E2**

More than just a place to sing, karaoke is also an excuse to let loose, a bonding ritual, a reason to keep the party going past the last train and a way to kill time until the first one starts in the morning. All parlours have private rooms equipped with decent audio-visual systems and a wide selection of songs in Japanese and English. Keen to recreate the scene in the film *Lost in Translation*? Book room 601 at **Karaoke-kan** *(karaokekan.jp)* on Center Gai.

Go to an Open Mic ENTERTAINMENT

If you happen to be a travelling artist who's itching to perform, a few live houses welcome visiting performers on open mic nights. Or simply go and watch to catch some local talent. **Black Bird Eatery** (MAP: 8 P84 **A1**; *blackbirdtokyo.com*) in Sasazuka hosts an open mic for acoustic musicians every fourth Friday of the month in a friendly community atmosphere (with homemade curry). In Ikenoue near Shimo-Kitazawa, at the smoky underground **Bar Gari Gari** (MAP: 9 P84 **C4**; *cinemabokan.com*), Joy and Sam host the monthly 'Drunk Poets' night for poetry in English, spoken or slammed, with occasional musical accompaniment. For the more comically inclined, **Tokyo Comedy Bar** (MAP: 10 P84 **E3**; *tokyocomedybar.com*) in the Renga building near Shibuya Station hosts regular 90-minute open mic line-ups of short (5-minute) stand-up acts in English and Japanese.

Listen to Jazz with a Japanese Twist LIVE MUSIC

Check out the schedules of independent live music venues around Shibuya and you might be surprised to find acts featuring traditional Japanese instruments playing in collaboration with more conventional jazz and classical instruments. At **Body & Soul** (MAP: 13 P84 **E1**; *bodyandsoul.co.jp*), a few times a year the flautist Kana

MUSIC KISSATEN

Lion

MAP: 11 P84 **D3**

No photography, no smoking, no talking, just the whispers of staff serving drinks at your table and the gentle clink of ice. Like a dimly lit church with giant wooden speakers instead of a pipe organ, projecting a gramophonic soundscape of soothing classical music. In Dōgen-zaka since 1926. Cash only. *(lion.main.jp; 1-8pm)*

Jazz & Coffee Masako

MAP: 12 P84 **B3**

Upstairs hideout in Shimo-Kitazawa, with an eclectic collection of vinyl records and an uninterrupted flow of jazz music. Great acoustics emitting from a wall of sound above vintage wooden furniture, figurines and beaded curtains. Serves single and blended coffee. *(instagram.com/jazzkissamasako; noon-10pm Fri-Wed, to 7.30pm Sun)*

Fuefuki leads a lively 'Shinobue Jazz' concert spotlighting her signature bamboo flutes, often with guest musicians playing a koto (zither) or *kotsuzumi* (hand drum). The hidden **Koen-Dori Classics** (MAP: 14 P84 **E2**; *koendori classics.com*) is a favourite venue of Yukihiro Issō, the legendary virtuoso player of the *nō* flute, who delights with his nimble-fingered improvisations and shocks with his experimental noise band. On a quiet hillside in Yoyogi Uehara, the concrete **Musicasa** (MAP: 15 P84 **A1**; *musicasa.co.jp*) classical concert hall has hosted performances by Earth Voice (*wadaiko* drumming plus singing and strumming on the rare Amami *sanshin*) and B-Come, an extraordinary ensemble of *biwa, shakuhachi* (bamboo flute), koto and percussion. Even the luxury jazz club **JZ Brat** (MAP: 16 P84 **E4**; *jzbrat.com*) has welcomed the jazz *shakuhachi* player Reikan Kobayashi.

Explore Subcultural Shimo-Kitazawa

SHOPPING

West of Shibuya, the bohemian enclave of **Shimo-Kitazawa** has its own distinct vibe. Home to writers and intellectuals since the 1920s, it attracted more artists, actors and musicians when several independent theatre companies were founded here in the 1980s. The neighbourhood gradually developed into the pedestrian-centred maze of fringe cafes and food shacks, vintage clothing and other thrift shops, independent live houses and arts venues that remains the core of Shimo-Kitazawa today.

One of these shops, **Flash Disc Ranch** (MAP: 17 P84 **B4**; *facebook.com/ flashdiscranch*), with its extensive collection of vintage vinyl records, was briefly featured in the 2024 film *Perfect Days* (look for the

colourful cartoon sign at the foot of the staircase). **Bear Pond Espresso** (MAP: 18 P84 **B3**; *bearpond espresso.com*), opened in 2009 by New York–trained and acclaimed barista Katsuyuki Tanaka, was featured in *A Film about Coffee*. Notwithstanding, Shimo-Kitazawa is perhaps best known in the mainstream for its well-stocked, smartly curated secondhand clothing shops, such as **Big Time** (MAP: 19 P84 **B3**; *bigtime.jp*), **Flamingo** (MAP: 20 P84 **B3**; *flamingo-online.jp*) and **Little Trip to Heaven** (MAP: 21 P84 **B3**; *littletriptoheaven.jp*).

Go Bar-Hopping in Ebisu

NIGHTLIFE

Downstream from Shibuya in all the right ways, Ebisu is full of side streets brimming with boutique bars, animated *izakaya* and many small restaurants. At **Bar Martha** (MAP: 22 P86 **D2**; *martha-records. com*), photography is prohibited, loud voices are discouraged and musical hegemony is enforced. Soulful songs on vinyl records from decades past are played on spot-lit turntables, amplified by giant vintage Tannoy speakers. For cocktails, try the fresh ginger Moscow Mule or the deliciously tangy Mango Mojito. On the other side of the railroad, little sister **Bar Track** (MAP: 23 P86 **D2**) offers a similar listening experience in a more intimate setting.

Ebisu is also known for its hidden bars, where simply finding the way in is already half the fun. **Janai Coffee** (MAP: 24 P86 C1; *janaicoffee.tokyo*) may be marked by a street-level sign, but it's fronted by a lower-basement decoy coffee stand that hides the passage into a classy speakeasy. Opposite Ebisu Park, pulling the handle of coin locker **A10** (MAP: 25 P86 C2; *a10club.jp*) opens the secret door to dark stairs leading down to the cocktail bar of the same name.

Indulge in Daikanyama SHOPPING

In the smart hills roughly triangulated by Shibuya, Ebisu and Meguro, **Daikanyama** sometimes feels like a private playground that you have the privilege of patronising. But the neighbourhood is built on many levels, both topographically and commercially, from the hillside **Log Road Daikanyama** (MAP: 26 P86 C1) strip that includes a brewpub and a doughnut shop, to the rolling mosaic of chic fashion and other independent boutiques around the area.

The open-air **T-Site** (MAP: 27 P86 B1; *store.tsite.jp*) complex is centred around the triple-block **Tsutaya Books** (MAP: 28 P86 B1) – which, in addition to lifestyle books, manga, international magazines and an executive lounge bar, dedicates an entire wall to luxury fountain pens. T-Site also includes a friendly e-bike shop, an organic health-food store and of course, a dog-grooming salon. It's one of the few places in Tokyo where you'll see Tesla chargers, not to mention someone casually walking their pet pig on a leash.

Stroll along the Meguro Riverside OUTDOORS

MAP: 29 P86 B2

The Meguro River is lined with cherry trees and in spring, many people stroll along the paved promenades under the boughs for *hanami* (cherry blossom viewing). At **Naka-Meguro**, the river narrows and the flowering trees form a tunnel of pink, framed by festive red lanterns above *sakura* petals floating downstream. The river thrums with chaotic yet joyful energy, as street vendors hawk everything from strawberry champagne to hot kebabs. This stretch is particularly dense with fashionable cafes, bars and boutiques – not to mention Tokyo's best-dressed dogs – making it a popular destination year-round.

In case you come during the off-season, the elegantly compact **Sato Sakura Museum** (*satosakura.jp; adult/child ¥800/free*) hosts a permanent collection of large-scale artworks that feature cherry blossoms in all their efflorescent glory, as well as related themed exhibitions of *nihonga* (Japanese paintings).

Best Places for...

Ɏ Budget   **ɎɎ** Midrange   **ɎɎɎ** Top End

Eating

Curry

Curry Spice Gelateria Kalpasi Ɏ

30 P84 **B4**

Flamboyant plates of curries, pickles and spices to be mixed into wild rice. Finish off with home-made gelato in herbal and creamy spicy-sweet flavours. *instagram.com/ kalpasi_shimokitazawa; 11.30am-9pm Fri-Wed*

Ten To Sen Spice Ramen Ɏ

31 P84 **B3**

Big bowls of thick, flavourful, spicy curry soup ramen overflowing with fresh vegetables, meats and burdock. *samurai-curry .com/tentosen; 11.30am-3pm & 5-8.30pm*

Noodles

Afuri Ɏ

32 P86 **D2**

The original location of this iconic ramen shop known for its yuzu salt broth. Also makes a tasty rainbow vegan ramen with colourful veg and roots. *afuri.com; 11am-5am*

Ramen Kamo To Negi ɎɎ

33 P84 **F3**

Wheat ramen bathing in a divine broth made from select Japanese 'duck and spring onions' that brings out the umami of the fine duck slices. *kamotonegi. com; 10am-4am*

Soba Maren Ɏ

34 P84 **D3**

Hole-in-the-wall for a rich bowl of soupless chewy soba topped with fresh ingredients such as lime and mint, with tender pork or chicken. *instagram.com/ soba_maren; 11.30am-11pm Sun-Thu, to 3am Fri-Sat*

Wagyū Burgers

Blacows ɎɎ

35 P86 **C1**

A fitting tribute to Japan's premium 'black cow' *wagyū* on 'B' branded buns. Gourmet toppings include gorgonzola with walnuts and fig sauce, pesto and more. *valuet.co .jp/brands/blacows; 11am-3pm & 5-9pm*

One-of-a-Kind

Shiro-hige's Cream Puff Factory Ɏ

36 P84 **A4**

Totoro-shaped cream puffs and cookies fill this Ghibli-approved bakery hidden in the forest near Shimo-Kitazawa. Go early, because they sell out of puffs almost every day. *shiro-hige.net; 10.30am-6pm Wed-Mon*

Shibuya Fureai Botanical Center Café ɎɎɎ

37 P84 **F4**

Home-brewed beverages and organic pizza, set inside the surreal environment of a multi-level community greenhouse. *sbgf.jp/cafe; 11am-9pm*

Hemp Café Tokyo ɎɎɎ

38 P86 **D1**

Casual joint serving surprisingly gourmet, elegantly presented CBD delicacies and vegan fare flavoured with homemade miso by a specialised chef. *hempcafetokyo.com; 11am-3pm & 6-10pm*

Fine Cuisine

d47 Shokudō ¥¥¥

39 P84 **F3**

Celebrating Japan's 47 prefectures with regional ingredients and homestyle specialties, overlooking Shibuya Station. *instagram .com/d47_shokudo; 11.30am-4pm & 6-9pm Thu-Tue*

Tofu Sorano ¥¥¥

40 P84 **F4**

Sumptuous dishes featuring homemade tofu with various sauces and spices, from steamed and silky to crispy deep-fried, in a small building full of cosy niches. *foodgate.net/shop/sorano; 5-10.45pm*

Thanks Nature ¥¥¥

41 P86 **C1**

Wholesome salads, thick smoothies and lovingly prepared fusion dishes using fresh vegetables and fine ingredients in a calm setting. *thanksnaturecafe. com; 11.30am-11pm*

Shopping

Souvenirs & Paper Goods

Loft

42 P84 **E2**

Stylish and affordable stationery, accessories and more. Browse the curated displays on the ground floor for gift-worthy Japanese souvenirs. *instagram .com/loft_shibuya; 11am-9pm*

Hands

43 P84 **E2**

Fun house for DIY hobbyists, analogue gamers, those seeking dog-sized Ohtani 17 baseball shirts and anyone who geeks out on 12 different brands of dental floss. *shibuya.hands. net; 10am-9pm*

Traveler's Factory

44 P86 **A2**

Niche shop in Naka-Meguro specialising in nostalgically retro travel accessories: paper notebooks, leather covers, pens, rubber stamps, Swiss Army knives... *travelers-factory. com; noon-8pm Wed-Mon*

Music

Tower Records

45 P84 **F2**

Eight packed floors of nonstop music, with listening stations. Note that this titanic Shibuya flagship, a rare successful vestige of the defunct US brand, dedicates its entire 6th floor to vinyl. *towershibuya. jp; 11am-10pm*

G'Club

46 P84 **E2**

Comprehensive new and used guitar store with an entire wall devoted to top brand ukuleles. There's even one autographed to the shop by Hawaiian ukulele virtuoso Jake Shimabukuro. *kurosawagakki.com/sh _gcshibuya; 11am-8pm, to 7pm Sun*

Books

Shibuya Publishing & Booksellers

47 P84 **D1**

Indie shop for art and illustrated books, Japanese lifestyle magazines and small-press publications, with a pop-up gallery space. *shibuyabooks.co.jp; 11am-9pm*

Flying Books

48 P84 **E3**

Vintage bookshop with a focus on counter-culture, visual and performing arts, magazines, collector's editions and other rare documents. *flying-books. com; 1-7pm*

Dogswear

Snobbish Babies

49 P86 **A1**

Mix-and-match frilly tops and bottoms, rubber socks and booties, backpacks and branded sweatshirts for your pooch, then buy yourself a blouse to match. *instagram .com/snobbishbabies _nakameguro; 11am-7pm*

See p113
for eating,
drinking and
shopping
listings

Takeshita Street

Explore
Harajuku & Aoyama

Researched by
Rob Goss

Harajuku (原宿) is Tokyo's famous fashion district, a fun place to shop, show off, get inspired or just hang out – there are lots of cool cafes and always a new restaurant or street food trend to try. The neighbourhood is bisected by a fashion-brand-lined boulevard called Omotesandō (表参道), with wide, tree-shaded pavements, while the side streets are a tangled maze where you'll find smaller, edgier boutiques and unique vintage stores. At the opposite end of Omotesandō is Aoyama (青山), a chic residential district with more cafes and boutiques, plus art venues such as the magnificent Nezu Museum.

Getting Around

 Train
Harajuku is one stop from Shibuya on the JR Yamanote line (and two stops from Shinjuku). The station, while small and easy to navigate, can get very crowded.

 Metro
There are two useful subway stations: Meiji-jingūmae (Chiyoda and Fukutoshin lines), which is adjacent to JR Harajuku Station, and Omotesandō (Chiyoda, Ginza and Hanzōmon lines) at the Aoyama end of the boulevard. Aoyama can also be accessed by Gaienmae Station on the Ginza line.

Walk
It's a 15- to 20-minute walk from Harajuku and Aoyama to Shibuya.

THE BEST

SHINTŌ SHRINE
Meiji-jingū (p103)

ART MUSEUM
Nezu Museum (p108)

GREEN SPACE
Yoyogi-kōen (p108)

CONTEMPORARY ARCHITECTURE
Omotesandō (p108)

SHOPPING STREET
Takeshita-dōri (p109)

Takeshita-dōri (p109)

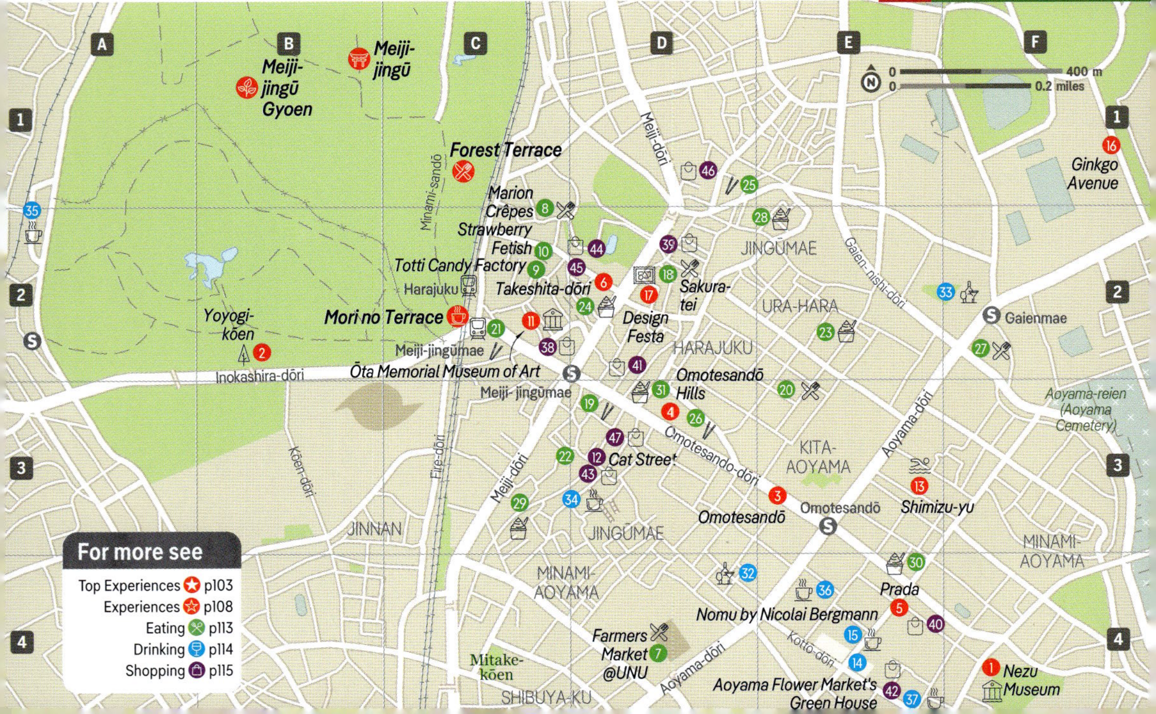

400 m
0.2 miles
N

Ginkgo Avenue

Aoyama-reien (Aoyama Cemetery)

MINAMI-AOYAMA

Gaienmae

Nezu Museum

Aoyama-dōri

Shimizu-yu

Prada

Nomu by Nicolai Bergmann

Aoyama Flower Market's Green House

Kotto-dōri

Gaien-nishi-dōri

JINGŪMAE

URA-HARA

HARAJUKU

KITA-AOYAMA

Omotesandō

Omotesandō Hills

Omotesandō-dōri

Sakura-tei

Design Festa

Meiji-dōri

Cat Street

JINGŪMAE

MINAMI-AOYAMA

Farmers Market @UNU

SHIBUYA-KU

Mitake-kōen

Forest Terrace

Marion Crêpes

Strawberry Fetish

Factory

Takeshita-dōri

Totti Candy Factory

Harajuku

Mori no Terrace

Meiji-jingūmae

Ōta Memorial Museum of Art

Meiji-jingū

Meiji-jingū Gyoen

Yoyogi-kōen

Inokashira-dōri

Minami-sandō

Fire-dōri

Kōen-dōri

JINNAN

Aoyama-dōri

For more see

Top Experiences p103
Experiences p108
Eating p113
Drinking p114
Shopping p115

Meiji-jingū

Meiji-jingū *(meijijingu.or.jp; free)* is considered a must-see – and it rarely disappoints. This monumental Shintō shrine made of unvarnished timber is ensconced in a 170-acre forest (bigger than Yoyogi-kōen). Popular with locals too, it's a great place to see, and take part in, traditional Japanese culture.

MAP P102 **B1**

Shrine in an Urban Forest

The entrance to Meiji-jingū is marked by the first of three towering *torii,* the elegant, somewhat pi-shaped gates that indicate the entrance to sacred Shintō ground. From here, a wide gravel path winds through a dense thicket of trees, taking about 15 minutes to reach the main sanctuary, a lantern-lit hall with a dramatic copper roof that occupies a clearing beyond the final, monumental gate.

While the whole scene appears timeless, Meiji-jingū is actually a relatively modern creation. Founded in 1920, it's dedicated to Emperor Meiji and Empress Shōken, whose reign (1868–1912) coincided with Japan's transformation from isolationist, feudal state to imperialist nation.

The forest is of similar vintage, created from hundreds of trees donated from all over Japan and planted by volunteers. Considered sacred and designed to flourish over generations, the forest has been left untouched ever since. For this reason, you can't stray from the path; you can, however, enjoy the literal breath of fresh air this rare urban forest provides.

PLANNING TIP
The shrine grounds are open from dawn (the garden, cafe and kiosks from 9am); the gates close at dusk – which in winter can be as early as 4pm.

Scan this QR code for shrine etiquette and other useful information.

PICTURESQUE JAPAN/SHUTTERSTOCK

Secret Garden

The grounds have an oft-overlooked garden, **Meiji-jingū Gyoen** (pictured above), which predates the founding of the shrine. Once part of a feudal estate, and later an imperial property, it has strolling paths, benches for contemplative breaks, and a pond with colourful koi and sunning turtles. A highlight is the iris garden; it's one of the personal touches added by Emperor Meiji, who designed it to please the empress. The couple often frequented the garden, which is cited as a reason for this location having been chosen for the shrine.

Admission to the garden is ¥500, which is why it is usually uncrowded – except in June when the irises bloom. Look for the entrance midway along the gravel path.

QUICK BREAK
There's a small cafe, **Mori no Terrace** (MAP P102 **C2**), at the entrance. More options can be found at the **Forest Terrace** (MAP P102 **C1**) complex before the second *torii* (on the right).

Visiting a Shintō Shrine

Shrines are part of the Shintō tradition, but are non-exclusive. There are no prohibitions on visiting, just an imperative to be respectful; this means refraining from behaviour that might be considered disruptive (such as eating, drinking, smoking or talking loudly). Photos are allowed, but not around the main hall or the kiosks, or of people praying.

There are a number of customs associated with visiting shrines; nothing is obligatory, but they can add to the experience and serve as a sign of respect. For example, just on your left before the final *torii*, there's a font, where it's customary to rinse your hands before entering the inner sanctuary. At the main hall, you can join visitors in greeting the *kami* (Shintō gods) with bows, hand claps and a small offering.

Votive Tablets & Amulets

To the right of the main sanctuary, you'll see racks of votive tablets – surrounding a magnificent camphor tree – on which messages are written. These are called *ema* and you can purchase them from the kiosks on the perimeter of the courtyard. Use one of the pens provided, then add your *ema* to the chorus of prayers, wishes and notes of gratitude in multiple languages.

The kiosks also sell *omamori* (amulets), silken pouches holding prayers for luck or protection. These might be for success in school entrance exams, safe childbirth, a happy union or safe travel. As Meiji-jingū is popular with international tourists, the amulets are labelled in English. Note that shrine (and temple) kiosks only accept cash – most tablets and amulets cost ¥1000 or ¥1500.

EVENTS AT MEIJI-JINGŪ
Meiji-jingū is an active religious site with a full calendar of rites, rituals and festivals. Twice a day, at 8am and 2pm, you can see the ceremonial offering of food and prayers to the *kami* (Shintō gods); check the calendar online for more events. This is also a popular place to get married; if you're lucky, you might even encounter a traditional wedding procession in the courtyard.

WALKING TOUR

Walk Harajuku

Harajuku rewards an early start: the earlier you can get to Meiji-jingū, the more serene the experience is likely to be. This also gives you plenty of time to hit more neighbourhood highlights, which include contemporary architecture, traditional art and trendy fashion. We've got advice for where to eat and drink along the way, too.

START	END	LENGTH
Harajuku Station	Takeshita-dōri	2km; 1½hr

1 After the Main Attraction

After an early-morning visit to **Meiji-jingū** (p103), walk through the urban forest to **Sarutahiko Coffee The Bridge** above JR Harajuku Station for a morning pick-me-up. The cafe opens at 8am and, despite being a chain, is known for meticulous pour-overs and espresso drinks made with single-origin beans.

2 Popular Photo Op

A couple of metres down the main road, at the Meiji-jingūmae intersection, there's no missing **Tokyu Plaza Omokado** with its hall-of-mirrors entrance, which has become a classic spot for an 'I'm in Harajuku' establishing shot. **Bills Omotesandō** (p113) is on the 7th floor, if you fancy brunch.

3 Designer Mall

Next up is a mall with a totally different look: **Omotesandō Hills** (p109), designed by famous architect Tadao Ando, is discreet in minimalist concrete and glass. Need a break? **Yasaiya Mei** (p113) and **Jean-Paul Hévin** (p114) are here.

4 Grand Boulevard

As you continue to stroll **Omotesandō** (p108), look out for more malls and shops with distinctive architecture. There's a nice vantage point of the boulevard from the pedestrian bridge, which you can use to cross the street.

5 Landmark Toy Store

On the left, as you return towards Harajuku, is famous toy store **Kiddy Land**. In business since 1950, it's part of Harajuku history, in addition to being a fun place to shop. The four-storey toy emporium has stationery, plushies and accessories featuring your Sanrio faves (Hello Kitty, Twin Stars, Rilakkuma), plus other cute character goods. If you need a lunch break, head to the casual dumpling restaurant **Harajuku Gyōza-rō** (p113), around the corner.

6 Trendsetting Department Store

Back at the Meiji-jingūmae intersection, head for famous Harajuku department store **Laforet** (p115), which carries high-street brands on the upper floors and more edgy offerings on the lower ones.

7 Unexpected Art Museum

Take the back exit, which puts you right in front of the **Ōta Memorial Museum of Art** (p110), which specialises in *ukiyo-e* (traditional woodblock prints). The small museum takes about an hour to tour.

8 Famous Fashion Street

Back into the thick of things, make your way up **Takeshita-dōri** (p111), Harajuku's signature shopping street – a place packed with stores selling vibrant youth fashions and all sorts of street snacks (p110).

EXPERIENCES

Stroll the Nezu Museum — MUSEUM

MAP: **1** P102 **F4**

Located in a quiet, residential pocket of Aoyama, **Nezu Museum** *(nezu-muse.or.jp; adult/child from ¥1300/¥1000)* houses the private collection of entrepreneur and art connoisseur Kaichirō Nezu (1860–1940), including premodern paintings, sculpture, lacquerware and ceramics from Japan, China and Korea. The museum first opened in 1941, though the current building – with its bamboo hedgerow and dramatic pitched roof – dates to the 2000s. It's the work of Kengo Kuma, the architect who designed the stadium for the 2020 Tokyo Olympics along with many other landmark buildings in Tokyo. The museum's garden, meanwhile, dates to the days of the original Nezu estate. Inspired by the aesthetics of the tea ceremony, it features flowing streams, rustic teahouses and antique stone lanterns. To extend the experience, head to the glass-walled Nezu Cafe – also designed by Kuma – for tea, coffee or lunch paired with garden views.

Join the Fun at Yoyogi-kōen — PARK

MAP: **2** P102 **B2**

If it's a sunny and warm weekend afternoon, you can count on there being a crowd lazing around the large grassy expanse that is **Yoyogi-kōen** *(tokyo-park.or.jp/park/yoyogi),* Tokyo's most popular public park. It might be a bit tatty compared to the city's more manicured gardens (and overrun with crows), but that's only because it gets so much use. This is where locals come to jog, walk their dogs and teach their kids how to ride bikes. It's an excellent place for a picnic and probably the only place in the city centre where you can reasonably toss a Frisbee without fear of hitting someone.

Across the road (use the overpass), there's a concrete plaza where events are held most weekends, especially during the warmer months. These include festivals celebrating the cultures and cuisines of Tokyo's foreign communities. Whatever's on, you can expect there to be *yatai* (food stalls) and crowds of revellers.

Spot the Works of Famous Architects on Omotesandō — ART & ARCHITECTURE

The last two decades have seen **Omotesandō** (MAP: **3** P102 **E3**), the boulevard connecting Harajuku and Aoyama, transformed by redevelopment. Today it's become a top destination for admiring contemporary architecture, since many of the designer boutiques were created by famous Japanese architects. There are buildings by SANAA (Dior), Toyō Ito (Bottega Veneta) and Jun Aoki (Louis Vuitton), all big names in the design world. Then there's the Tadao Ando-designed **Omotesandō Hills** (MAP: **4** P102 **D3**), which runs 250m along the street and the interior of which is a fine example of Ando's sleekly minimalist approach. Each building has a signature look, achived with innovative materials and structural design, which gives you a feel for the architect's style. If you continue into Aoyama, you can see more interesting buildings, such as Herzog & de Meuron's iconic design for **Prada** (MAP: **5** P102 **E4**).

See Harajuku's Style History on Takeshita-dōri

FASHION

MAP: **6** P102 **D2**

Takeshita-dōri (*takeshita-street. com*) is best known as the locus of the goth and Lolita scenes that flourished in the early 2000s. But it's no one-hit-wonder: for half a century, this meandering lane – lined with small boutiques and free of car traffic – has been a beacon of creative style. Other looks incubated here include the rainbow-bright, super-*kawaii* (cute) 'decora' style that ruled Harajuku in the 1990s.

While nowadays most fashion scenes are online, Takeshita-dōri remains a pilgrimage site for teens from all over Japan, and it can get absolutely jammed in the afternoons. Remnants of fashion trends past can be found here and there, alongside more contemporary shops. Still committed to being extra, it's an especially good place to shop for fun accessories (like animal-shaped backpacks) and colourful basics such as socks and tights. As much a place to hang out as shop, in the past decade it's also become the place to sample the latest trends in sweets and street food.

Hang Out at the Farmers Market

MARKETS

MAP: **7** P102 **D4**

Farmers markets can be a great way to get to know a city and

— **HARAJUKU PAST & PRESENT** —

Until the 20th century, Harajuku was little more than a village. Meiji-jingū changed that, but so did WWII. During the US occupation that followed, something like an American suburb for servicemen and their families went up in what is now Yoyogi-kōen – an exotic sight but one closed to ordinary Japanese. Then in the 1970s, when part of Omotesandō was still closed to car traffic on Sundays, came a new twist: Tokyo youth began spontaneously gathering to dance in the street, many dressed in flamboyant outfits purchased on Takeshita-dōri – setting in motion the neighbourhood's transformation into trendsetting fashion centre, a reputation that lasts to this day.

TAKESHITA-DŌRI STREET FOOD

Takeshita-dōri is one of the few places in Tokyo with a thriving street-food scene, and the specialities are as sweet as they come.

Marion Crêpes

MAP: **8** P102 **C2**

Crêpes stuffed with whipped cream and sliced fruit are classic Harajuku – and Marion Crêpes is the classic place to get them (*marion.co.jp; 10am-9pm*)

Totti Candy Factory

MAP: **9** P102 **C2**

Totti's magnificent (and photogenic) rainbow candy-floss swirls are part of the new wave of Takeshita-dōri sweets (*totticandy. com; 10am-7pm Mon-Fri, 9am-8pm Sat & Sun*)

Strawberry Fetish

MAP: **10** P102 **C2**

The latest sweet to take Harajuku by storm is *tanghulu* – skewers of glossy, sugar-glazed fruit, a sweet treat from China (*strawberryfetish. com; 10am-8pm Mon-Fri, from 9am Sat & Sun*)

Tokyo is no exception. One of the city's best, and longest running, takes place in the plaza that fronts the United Nations University (UNU) campus on Aoyama-dōri. As well as stalls selling organic vegetables, jams, honey and baked goods, this is also where you'll find some Tokyo's best food trucks and food-related events, which contribute a festival-like atmosphere to the whole scene.

The **Farmers Market @UNU** (*farmersmarkets.jp; free*) is held at weekends from 10am to 4pm. Come for the great vibes and stay for the chance to chat with vendors and learn more about Japan's local food culture.

Detour to the Ōta Memorial Museum of Art

ART & ARCHITECTURE

MAP: **11** P102 **C2**

The **Ōta Memorial Museum of Art** (*ukiyoe-ota-muse.jp; adult/ child from ¥1000/free*) is among the best places in the city to see *ukiyo-e*, a style of woodblock printing popularised in the Edo period (1603–1868). Prints often depict scenes from the era – its courtesans, kabuki actors and cherry-blossom parties – and always in vivid colour. About 100 works from the museum's extensive collection are displayed at a time in themed, often seasonal, exhibitions.

Cool and dark, save for the spotlights on the works, the museum is a welcome respite from busy Harajuku. Upon entering, you're required to swap your street shoes for slippers, like at a traditional inn. The museum is closed on Mondays and between exhibitions.

Scout New Looks in Ura-Hara

FASHION

MAP: **12** P102 **D3**

Want to dig deeper into the Harajuku fashion scene? After you've strolled Takeshita-dōri, continue on to 'Ura-Hara' – the nickname for the warren of unnamed backstreets behind Omotesandō. This is where you'll find the upstart brands and secondhand stores from which Harajuku's current generation of trendsetters cobble together their head-turning looks.

One place to set your sights on is 6% Doki Doki (p115) , which has *kawaii* (cute) accessories and an easy-to-spot, bubble-gum-pink building. On the opposite side of Omotesandō, check out **Cat Street**, another pedestrianised street that's lined with shops; it has a mix of big brands, small boutiques and recycle shops, including RagTag (p115).

Clean Up at a Neighbourhood Bathhouse

LOCAL CULTURE

MAP: **13** P102 **E3**

Curious to dip your toe into Japanese bathing culture? Consider visiting a neighbourhood *sentō* (public bathhouse). Once a staple of Tokyo life, though less common today now that homes have their own bathrooms, these have big, communal tubs for deep, long (and hot!) soaks. While out and about in Aoyama, you could drop by

Shimizu-yu (*shimizuyu.jp; adult/ child from ¥550/¥200),* a *sentō* with a crisp, modern look and a variety of amenities, including rain showers, jet baths and two saunas. Given that *sentō* are traditionally no-frills bathhouses where locals come with their own soap and towels, you'll need to pack wash gear or pay extra for the 'sauna course with rental towels' *(¥1330),* which will give you access to everything plus essentials such as soap and shampoo.

As for bathing etiquette, the most important thing to know is that you need to clean up at the showers and rinse well *before* getting into the soaking tubs. Shimizu-yu is open from noon until midnight *(until 11pm at weekends)* and closed on Fridays. Visitors with tattoos are not allowed entry.

Have Tea in a Flower Shop

TEA & COFFEE

Fashionable Aoyama has not one but two flower shops with tea salons attached, and they make for a lovely break from the urban world outside. At **Aoyama Flower Market's Green House** (MAP: **14** P102 **E4**; *afm-teahouse.com/aoyama)* foliage drips from the ceiling and down the walls, while flowerbeds run under the glass-top tables, all of which are topped with vases holding fragrant, fresh-cut blooms. Menu highlights include teas made

GOLDEN GINKGOS

Tokyo's official tree is the ginkgo, called *ichō* in Japanese – once you realise this, you'll see the motif of the fan-shaped leaves everywhere. For a couple of weeks around late November and early December, the trees turn a dazzling shade of yellow and carpet the pavements in gold when the leaves fall. The most famous display is along the aptly named **Ginkgo Avenue** *(Ichō-namiki)* in Aoyama, near Gaienmae subway station. Another good local spot is along the western edge of Yoyogi-kōen, near Yoyogi-kōen subway station.

MAP: **16** P102 **F1**

with fresh herbs, dried flowers and natural aromatics, served by the pot, plus one of the prettiest parfaits in Tokyo.

If the queue for that is long, then you could instead head a street away to **Nomu** (MAP: **15** P102 **E4**; *nicolaibergmannnomu.com*), produced by Danish flower artist Nicolai Bergmann. His signature flower boxes, which are popular gifts in Tokyo, are on display in the shop area, along with bouquets in bold shades. The adjoining salon is bright and spacious, with seasonal flower art decorating the walls and a menu full of Scandinavian flavours – that includes a *smørrebrød* sandwich plate and Nordic banana cake, plus a selection of loose-leaf teas from Danish purveyor AC Perch's.

Check Out What's Happening at Design Festa

ART & ARCHITECTURE

Design Festa (MAP: **17** P102 **D2**; *designfestagallery.com; free*) has long been a champion of Tokyo's DIY art scene and its maze-like building is a Harajuku landmark. The building is a work of art in its own right, and is always changing. Inside there are dozens of small galleries rented by the day. More often than not, the artists themselves are hanging around, too. Pair a visit with a meal at *okonomiyaki* (savoury pancakes) restaurant **Sakura-tei** (MAP: **18** P102 **D2**; *sakuratei.co.jp*) which is part of the complex. Here you can grill your own *okonomiyaki*, and there are options for vegetarians and kids.

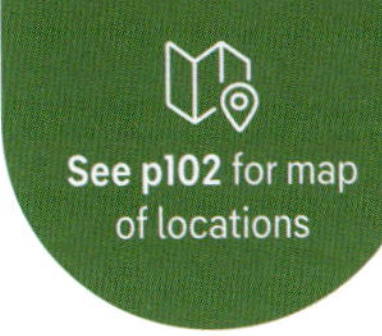

Best Places for...

 Budget    Midrange   Top End

Eating

Japanese Comfort Food

Harajuku Gyōza-rō 

19   **D3**

Long-running favourite for all-day plates of *gyōza* (dumplings), served *yaki* (fried) or *sui* (boiled). There's often a queue but service moves quickly. *11.30am-10pm*

Maisen

20   **E3**

Famed both for its *tonkatsu* (breaded, deep-fried pork cutlets) and its setting (an old public bathhouse). If you can't get a seat, the takeaway window sells delicious *tonkatsu* sandwiches. *mai-sen.com; 11am-9pm*

Kyūshū Jangara

21   **C2**

Come sample the thin noodles, tender *chāshū* (roast pork) and rich broth for which Kyūshū-style ramen is famous. There's a decent vegan version, too. *kyushujangara.co.jp; 10am-10pm*

Pancakes & Crêpes

Micasadeco & Cafe

22   **C3**

One of the most popular places to try super-fluffy soufflé pancakes, one of the most popular things to eat in Harajuku. It's small, so expect to queue. *micasadecoandcafe.com; 11am-5pm Mon-Fri, 10am-6pm Sat & Sun*

Breizh Café Crêperie

23   **E2**

If Takeshita-dōri's cream-filled crêpes had you craving authentic, French galettes, you're in luck because Harajuku has those, too. *le-bretagne .com/creperie/omotes ando; 11am-10.30pm Mon-Fri, 9am-9.30pm Sat & Sun*

Bills Omotesandō

24   **D2**

Try the ricotta hotcakes (with fresh banana and honeycomb butter) at this beachy Australian import that started the trend for all-day pancakes in Harajuku. *billsjapan.com; 8.30am-10pm*

Organic & Macrobiotic

Mominoki House

25   **D1**

Highlights at this historic macrobiotic restaurant include the vegan sushi made with brown rice (served only at dinner). *mominoki-house.net; 11am-3pm & 5-11pm Mon-Fri, to 10pm Sat & Sun*

Yasaiya Mei

26   **D3**

Farm-fresh organic vegetables presented in myriad ways, including crudités styled like a bouquet; note that not all meal sets are vegetarian. Inside Omotesandō Hills. *omotesandohills.com; 11am-10.30pm Sun-Thu, to 11pm Fri & Sat*

Citron

27   **F2**

Flavourful salads, quiches and gratins made by a French chef – all organic and vegetarian. Try the onion quiche, with lovely hints of rosemary and caramelisation. *citron. co.jp; 8am-9pm Mon-Fri, to 7pm Sat & Sun*

Sweet Treats

Muun Seoul Café 

28 E2

The place to get Korean-style chunky macarons in pretty pastel shades, paired with equally dreamy beverages such as strawberry milk and mixed berry soda. *11am-7pm*

Initial 

29 C3

Decadent parfaits in sculptural arrangements, created with seasonal fruit and rich soft-serve made from Hokkaidō cream; gelato and fruit sandwiches, too. *noon-10pm Mon-Fri, from 11am Sat & Sun*

Higashiya Man

30 E4

Mid-shop Aoyama pitstop for fresh-steamed *manjū* (buns stuffed with sweet red bean paste), plus traditional Japanese sweets packaged as gifts. Counter service only. *higashiya.com/shop/ man; 11am-7pm*

Jean-Paul Hévin

31 D3

Sip rich, gourmet hot chocolate on the ground floor of stylish mall Omotesandō Hills while looking dreamily out the window. *omotesandohills. com; 11am-8pm*

Drinking

Cocktails & Mocktails

Two Rooms

32 D4

Martinis, mojitos, mocktails and smoothies, plus sweeping views over Harajuku – if you can score a seat on the terrace. Also good for a boozy brunch. *tworooms. jp; 11.30am-2am Mon & Tue, to 3am Wed-Sat, to midnight Sun*

PR Bar

33 F2

Vintage bar vibes, classic cocktails (like negronis and grasshoppers) and a deep collection of spirits, including lots of Japanese gin. *prbar-rebirth-project.therestaurant.jp; 7pm-1am Mon-Sat*

Coffee

Roastery by Nozy

34 D3

Espresso drinks made from beans carefully sourced and roasted in-house, right on Cat Street. Another reason to stop by: the espresso-flavoured soft-serve. *tysons.jp/roastery; 10am-10pm*

Little Nap Coffee Stand

35 A2

Located alongside Yoyogi-kōen, this delightful pocket cafe serves strong coffee brews and baked goods. The machiato is fantastic. *littlenap.jp; 9am-7pm*

Japanese Tea

Sakurai Japanese Tea Experience

36 E4

Chic contemporary salon serving tea sets paired with traditional sweets by day and, after 7pm on weekdays, original cocktails made with tea. Reservations recommended. *sakurai-tea.jp; 11am-11pm Mon-Fri, to 8pm Sat & Sun*

Matsubaya Saryō

37 E4

Teashop on Kotto-dōri that blends traditional and modern aesthetics, with dark interiors and bonsai on the tables, while serving a variety of high-grade Japanese teas and sweets. *mtbysr.jp; 10am-6pm*

Shopping

Local Landmarks

Laforet
38 C2

Iconic Harajuku department store carrying trendy high-street fashions, up-and-coming Japanese brands and goth looks (the latter in the basement, naturally). *laforet.ne.jp; 11am-8pm*

Beams Harajuku
39 D2

Long-running, trendsetting Meiji-dōri menswear boutique; it's now a national chain, but this is the original. Nearby, look for spin-off shops for womenswear, graphic T-shirts and more. *beams. co.jp; noon-8pm Mon-Fri, from 11am Sat & Sun*

Unique Boutiques

Reality Lab Issey Miyake
40 E4

The latest, innovative creations from legendary Japanese fashion house Issey Miyake, in a futuristic space designed by artist and designer Tokujin Yoshioka. *isseymiyake.com; 11am-8pm*

6% Doki Doki
41 D2

Acid-bright fashion and accessories that are part raver, part schoolgirl and, according to the shop's name, '6% exciting' (and 100% Harajuku). *6dokidoki.com; 1-7pm Mon-Fri, from noon Sat & Sun*

Sou-Sou
42 E4

Clothes and accessories that riff on traditional styles, including *jika-tabi* – the rubber-soled, split-toed shoes worn by construction workers in Japan – in colourful prints. *sousou.co.jp; noon-8pm*

Secondhand & Resell

RagTag
43 D3

Big (by Tokyo standards) consignment shop stocked with labels Harajuku shoppers love, like Comme des Garçons and Vivienne Westwood. On Cat Street. *ragtag.jp; 11am-8pm*

Closet Child
44 D2

The best resell shop for goth and Lolita styles, including gently used pieces from Emily Temple cute, Milk and more. On Takeshita-dōri. *cc.closet-child.info; 4-7pm Mon-Wed & Fri-Sat*

Chicago
45 D2

Basement vintage shop on Takeshita-dōri with racks of inexpensive, secondhand kimonos, *yukata* (light cotton robes), obi (sashes) and more. Also has other branches in the neighbourhood. *chicago.co.jp; 10am-8pm*

Traditional Crafts & Souvenirs

Musubi
46 D1

Impressively versatile (and environmentally friendly), *furoshiki* are traditional cloths that can be folded and knotted to form shopping bags, wrap gifts and more. Find them here in classic and contemporary designs. *musubi-furoshiki.com; 11am-7pm Thu-Tue*

Oriental Bazaar
47 D3

If the name seems dated that's because it's among Harajuku's oldest souvenir shops, starting out as an antiques dealer and now in a new location. *orientalbazaar.co.jp; 11am-6.30pm Fri-Tue*

See p130
for eating,
drinking and
shopping
listings

Explore
Shinjuku & West Tokyo

Researched by
Louise George Kittaka

On one side of Shinjuku (新宿) are office buildings and high-rises; on the other are shopping malls and neon-lit streets. Things only quieten down when the trains stop running in the wee small hours, though the parties continue in bars and clubs. Amid this bustle, you'll also find spacious parks offering a breath of fresh air.

A short train ride takes you to Nakano (中野) and Kōenji (高円寺), two laid-back West Tokyo neighbourhoods with eclectic shops and thrift stores. The Nakano Broadway mall offers anime merchandise stores and arcades.

Getting Around

 **Train**

The JR Yamanote, Chūō-Sōbu, Odakyū and Keiō lines stop at Shinjuku. The Chūō line stops at Nakano and the Sōbu line stops at Kōenji.

 **Metro**

Shinjuku Station is served by the Marunouchi, Toei Ōedo and Toei Shinjuku lines. The Marunouchi, Fukutoshin and Toei Shinjuku lines stop at Shinjuku-sanchōme Station, connected to Shinjuku Station via underpass.

 **Walk**

Kōenji is about a 20-minute walk west from Nakano.

THE BEST

CHERRY BLOSSOMS
Shinjuku-gyoen (p120)

IZAKAYA
Omoide-yokochō (p126)

ANIME & MANGA
Nakano Broadway (p121)

BAR-HOPPING
Golden Gai (p122)

LGBTIQ+ NIGHTLIFE
Shinjuku Nichōme (p127)

Shinjuku skyline (p124)
SEAN PAVONE/SHUTTERSTOCK

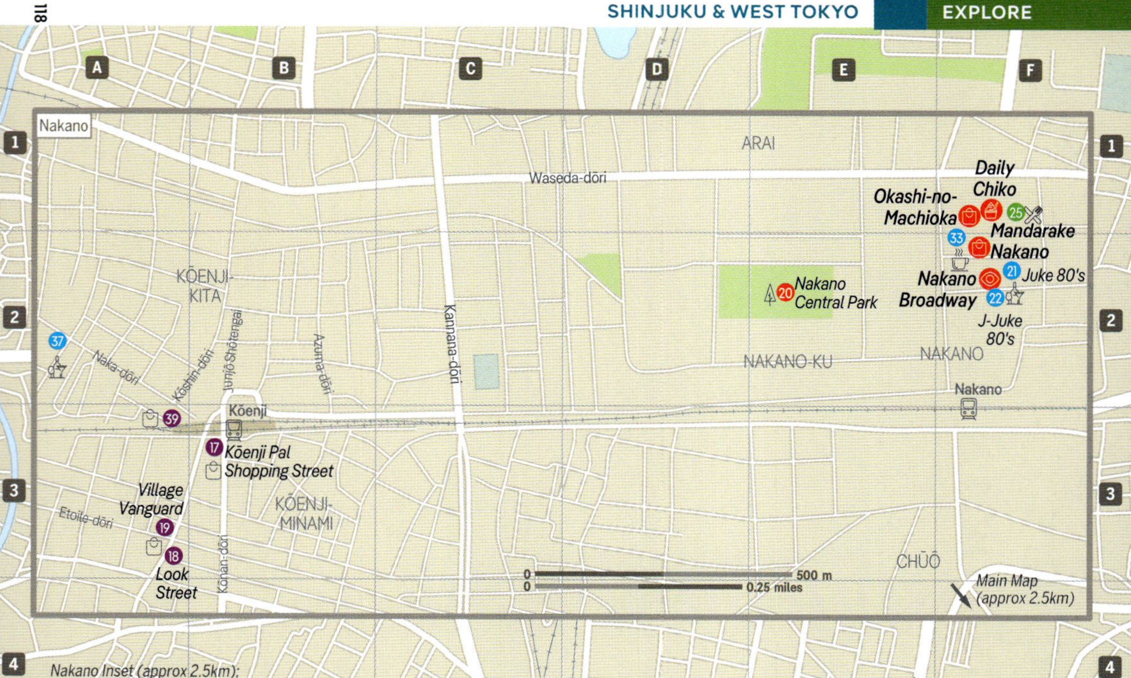
Nakano
A
B
C
D
E
F
1
2
3
4
ARAI
Waseda-dōri
Daily Chiko
Okashi-no-Machioka
25
Mandarake
33
Nakano
Nakano Broadway
21
Juke 80's
22
J-Juke 80's
20
Nakano Central Park
NAKANO-KU
NAKANO
Nakano
KŌENJI-KITA
37
Naka-dōri
Kōshin-dōri
Junjō Shōtengai
Azuma-dōri
Kannana-dōri
Kōenji
39
17
Kōenji Pal Shopping Street
Village Vanguard
KŌENJI-MINAMI
Etoile-dōri
19
Konan-dōri
18
Look Street
CHŪŌ
0   500 m
0   0.25 miles
Main Map (approx 2.5km)
Nakano Inset (approx 2.5km); Ghibli Museum, Mitaka (12km)
KABUKICHŌ
Meiji-dōri

Ōme-kaidō
Central Rd
Golden Gai
Subnade
Ramen Nagi
SHINJUKU-KU
Shinjuku-nishiguchi
Omoide-yokochō
Yasukuni-dōri
Shinjuku
Bic Camera
Isetan
Gyoen-dōri
Yasukuni-dōri
Kita-dōri
Bar
Adezakura
Aiiro Cafe
Goldfinger
AiSOTOPE Lounge
NISHI-SHINJUKU
Shinjuku
Lumine EST
Shinjuku-sanchōme
Shinjuku-sanchōme
SHINJUKU
Arty Farty
Eagle Tokyo Blue
Tochōmae
Tokyo Metropolitan Government Building
Dragon Men
SHINJUKU-NICHŌME
Kōen-dōri
Tochō-dōri
Gijido-dōri
Season Rd
Shinjuku Station
Shinjuku-dōri
Shinjuku Chūō-kōen
Shinjuku-gyoenmae
Shinjuku
National Parks Discovery Centre
NEWoMan
Takashimaya Times Square
One Day's St
Kōshū-kaidō
YOYOGI
Hands
Meiji-dōri
Books Kinokuniya Tokyo
Shinjuku-gyoen
SHIBUYA-KU
Kyū-Goryō-tei
Yoyogi
400 m
0.2 miles
For more see
Top Experiences p120
Experiences p126
Eating p130
Drinking p130
Shopping p131

★ **TOP EXPERIENCE**

Shinjuku-gyoen

Centred in perhaps one of Tokyo's busiest neighbourhoods is Shinjuku-gyoen *(adult/child ¥500/free),* a former feudal lord's residence turned imperial garden before its doors opened to the public in 1951. It is now a welcome oasis for city-dwellers to stroll through its peaceful gardens and shelter under the trees.

MAP P118 **F8**

PLANNING TIP
Advance online ticket reservations with a designated entry time may be required during peak cherry-blossom season (March to April). Tickets can be purchased at the gate any other time of the year.

Scan this QR code for information and to book tickets online.

The Gardens

The park has three distinct garden styles – French formal, English landscape and Japanese traditional – and a perfect day in Shinjuku begins with a morning stroll along the winding paths where the gardens unfold. Seasonal blooms colour the park at any given time of year, but the prettiest is the cherry-blossom season, when the sakura trees and the ground below are blanketed in pink petals. For the locals, this is also the time for *hanami,* or cherry-blossom-viewing parties at the park.

Landmarks of Shinjuku-gyoen

In the Japanese traditional garden is **Kyū-Goryō-tei**, or the Taiwan Pavilion, gifted to commemorate the wedding of then-Crown Prince Hirohito. A rare example of traditional Chinese architecture in Japan, it is also the only structure that survived WWII air raids in the decade following the time it was built. Don't miss the orchids blooming inside the greenhouse too.

On your way out, stop by the **National Parks Discovery Centre** (located inside the Information Centre; MAP P118 **F7**) to see the interactive and projection-mapped displays and stunning images of national parks across the country.

Nakano Broadway

Fans of anime and manga tend to flock to the geeky neighbourhood of Akihabara (p137), but Nakano Broadway offers a great taster for those short on time, or who want a multifaceted look into some of Tokyo's subcultures all within a retro shopping complex.

MAP P118 **F2**

Comics & Collectibles

The main draw is the array of shops stocked with shelves of manga (Japanese comics), and every anime and character merchandise available – from plushies and figurines to tableware. Popular manga and collectible store **Mandarake Nakano** has outlets across all the upper four floors of the complex. But that's not all – porcelain dolls, railway memorabilia, books, limited-edition items and vintage watches are just a fraction of what you'll find here. There's even a secondhand kimono store alongside produce and teashops in the basement.

Fun & Games

There are two excellent arcades in the building: Adores and Namco. Adores is near the entrance and has crowd-pleasing crane games and Mario Kart, but rhythm game enthusiasts and those looking for more game varieties will enjoy Namco, tucked in a corner of the ground floor.

Don't leave Nakano Broadway without getting the comically large, eight-layer soft serve from **Daily Chiko** (MAP P118 **F1**) in the basement. And if you really have a thing for Japanese snacks, fill up your shopping basket at bargain sweet store **Okashi-no-Machioka** (MAP P118 **F1**), where prices are comparable to discount store Don Quijote.

PLANNING TIP
The closest station is Nakano Station, a four-minute train ride from Shinjuku Station on the JR Chūō Line rapid service. Many shops here tend to close on Wednesdays. Weekends get crowded.

Scan this QR code for information about Nakano Broadway.

Golden Gai & Kabukichō

Tokyo's most famous (or infamous) nightlife district is right here in Shinjuku. There are two main areas: Golden Gai and Kabukichō. The former is a corner of Shinjuku lined with tiny bars and the latter is the glorious, neon-lit wonderland that the neighbourhood is renowned for.

MAP P118 **E5**

PLANNING TIP

Bars in Shinjuku only start filling up from 9pm and may stay open until 5am or 6am. Trains do not run 24 hours – if you miss the last one, catch the first train the next day or take a taxi.

Scan this QR code for information on Golden Gai.

Night Life in Kabukichō

By day, Kabukichō (*kabukicho.or.jp*) is an average part of town that sometimes looks a bit quiet and sparse, but nightfall is when it truly shines – quite literally. Tokyoites come here to unwind under the neighbourhood's neon-lit glow on Friday evenings and at weekends, dropping into the area's many *izakaya* (Japanese pub-eateries) and bars.

Though brightly lit, there can be a rather seedy veneer to the area that can seem daunting, but most bars here are fine. However, Kabukichō is a red-light district and it's always a good idea to check a bar's reviews on Google prior to going, just as an extra precaution. Touts are common in the area and are best ignored, as those bars tend to overcharge.

Karaoke is a popular evening pastime here and all-night karaoke boxes are dotted around the area if you're looking to do some serious singing. Evening rates typically start at ¥500 per half hour.

The Many Faces of Golden Gai

Golden Gai (*gai* means street; pictured right) is a quieter area just beside Kabukichō that is known for its narrow lanes lined with dingy, atmospheric bars – hundreds of them. Bars here typically fit no

RICHIE CHAN/SHUTTERSTOCK

more than a dozen people and a visit to the ones on the top floor typically involves a precarious climb up a cramped and creaky wooden staircase. If you love themed bars and intimate settings, you could spend the entire night here hopping from one bar to another – some covered in retro movie posters, some sleek and modern.

Cover Charges

Bar-hopping does not come cheap, however. Some places ask for a cover charge *(¥500 to ¥1500)* and drinks are typically ¥700 and up. Because the selection of bars here is so diverse, your experience may also vary greatly – some bars will waive the cover charge for tourists, but some may deny entry to tourists entirely. Many bars are also cash-only, so make sure you have enough on hand.

QUICK BREAK
Complete your night out with a bowl of rich, savoury ramen at popular **Ramen Nagi**, located on the 1st floor of one of the buildings in Golden Gai – look for the round lantern out front. Open 24 hours.

Walk Shinjuku

Shinjuku is split into two distinct areas. To the west are hotels, high-rise offices and a city park; to the east is a world of nighttime entertainment, shopping and some cultural sights in between. The east side truly comes alive at night, so come in the late afternoon to catch all the sights at their best.

START	END	LENGTH
Tokyo Metropolitan Government Building	Isetan	4km; 2hr

1 Shinjuku from the Top

The **Tokyo Metropolitan Government Building** (p126) can be reached from the west exit of Shinjuku Station either above ground, or via an underpass (follow signs from the station). Completed in 1990, this is one of the city's most recognisable buildings. On the top floor in each tower are observation decks that are free to access.

2 The City Park

A small patch of green across the road is **Shinjuku Chūō Park**. Well-manicured lawns and plenty of seating make this park a great place to sit and take in the Shinjuku cityscape. There are also a few cafes to sit in or to buy a coffee to enjoy on the grass.

3 Eat Street

Double back towards Shinjuku Station, passing by the neighbourhood's hotels and high-rises. Head north towards **Omoide-yokochō** (p126), a cramped alleyway that was a postwar black market, but is now lined with *izakaya*. Though mostly closed by day, the shops here dole out frothy beers and *yakitori* (skewered meat) at nightfall.

4 A Shinjuku Icon

Take the underpass beneath the train tracks and you'll come to Cross Space Shinjuku, on top of which is a 3D billboard sometimes featuring cats and popular characters. Head north down Shinjuku Moa 2 Ave and you'll start to see the **Godzilla Head**, eyes aglow and peeking out from behind Toho Cinemas – the bright centre of Kabukichō.

5 Kabukichō's Shrine

Go east from here, passing through the red-light district of Kabukichō and the small shanty bars of Golden Gai, eventually coming to **Hanazono-jinja**. Founded in the 17th century, the Shintō shrine is dedicated to Inari, god of agriculture and prosperity. A flea market is held here on Sundays.

6 A Sweet Break

Get onto Meiji-dōri and continue straight towards the department store **Isetan** (p128). Opened in 1933, the building retains its grand classic facade. Inside are fashion-forward boutiques, high-end brands and a variety of restaurants and cafes. In the basement is perhaps the neighbourhood's best gourmet food hall, with beautiful chocolates and confectionery in gleaming glass cases, plus other mouthwatering offerings.

EXPERIENCES

Admire the Cityscape

OBSERVATION DECK

MAP: **1** P118 **A6**

At 242.9m tall, the **Tokyo Metropolitan Government Building** (*zaimu.metro.tokyo.lg.jp/tochousha/goannai; free*) is among the tallest buildings in the city. But unlike the commercial skyscrapers where visitors have to fork out for a ticket, you can get the same sweeping views at the observatory atop the two towers here, entirely free of charge. From the south observatory (*open 9.30am to 10pm*) you'll be able to spot Mt Fuji in the distance on clear days. The night views from here – which will include a beautifully lit Tokyo Skytree – are spectacular.

If you're in Shinjuku for the evening, keep an eye on the building, which becomes a canvas for the world's largest projection-mapped display featuring some of Tokyo's icons and scenes from nature. The show takes place nightly from 7pm (though the schedule may change depending on the season) and different artworks are featured at weekends.

Tochōmae Station on the Toei Ōedo line is closest to the Tokyo Metropolitan Government Building.

Kanpai at the Izakaya

DINING

MAP: **2** P118 **C5**

A place to stay and drink alcohol – that's what *izakaya* roughly translates as. Often referred to as a Japanese bar or tavern, the *izakaya* is a mainstay of Japanese society. It's where friends and colleagues come together and chat over drinks, food and the sound of clinking glasses, accompanied with shouts of *'Kanpai!'* (Cheers!)

In Shinjuku, **Omoide-yokochō** (*en.shinjuku-omoide.com*) and Ka-bukichō are where you'll find the largest concentration of *izakaya*. Locals typically go to an *izakaya* after work for dinner and drinks, downing mugs of cheap beer and eating sticks of *yakitori* (grilled chicken skewers). If you're looking to get buzzed for cheap, *izakaya* have you covered too with their two-hour alcoholic all-you-can-drink plans available all night, called *nomihōdai*.

It's a good idea to go early (before 7pm) as *izakaya* can get quite busy and large groups may want to make a reservation. Most *izakaya* take a seating charge per person (between ¥500 and ¥800) and in return guests are served an appetiser, known as *otōshi*. When looking for an *izakaya*, avoid the touts at Kabukichō to prevent being overcharged. Opt for well-known chains with transparent pricing, or check reviews online beforehand.

Party in Nichōme   LGBTIQ+ DISTRICT

Shinjuku Nichōme, colloquially known as 'Nichōme' or 'Nichō', is Tokyo's largest nightlife area specifically catered to the LGBTIQ+ community. About a 10-minute walk from Shinjuku's Golden Gai, the area was a red-light district during Japan's postwar years and when sex work was outlawed in 1958, gay bars began taking over the premises that were once occupied by brothels. The exact number is up for debate, but it is believed that up to 500 bars now occupy this 300-sq-metre area.

There are a number of well-known bars here that are hotspots for locals, expats and tourists: **Aiiro Cafe** (MAP: ③ P118 **F6**; *aliving .net/aiirocafe*) is one of Nichōme's most popular, staffed by friendly, international members of the community and offering all-you-can-drink beer at happy hour for the unbeatable price of ¥1000. If you don't know where to start in Nichōme, this is a good place to mingle with both locals and expats and get to know the area. For the ladies, **Bar Goldfinger** (MAP: ④ P118 **F6**; *linktr.ee/goldfingertokyo*) and **Adezakura** (MAP: ⑤ P118 **F6**; *adezaku ra.tokyo*) are open exclusively to women at weekends – Goldfinger also has free popcorn and karaoke. For go-go boys, drag queens, bear or K-pop nights and themed events, check out what's happening at weekends at **AiSOTOPE Lounge** (MAP: ⑥ P118 **F6**; *aisotope-lounge.net*) or **Eagle Tokyo Blue** (MAP: ⑦ P118 **F6**; *eagletokyo.com*). For a night of dancing, head to **Dragon Men** (MAP: ⑧ P118 **E6**; *instagram .com/dragon.men*) or **Arty Farty** (MAP: ⑨ P118 **E6**; *artyfarty.jp*). The evening typically starts to get lively after 8pm and most of the popular

THE NOSTALGIA OF OMOIDE-YOKOCHŌ

Omoide-yokochō presents a passage into the past. With its dim, lantern-lit alleys crammed with shops and *izakaya* that haven't changed for at least half a century, it's a rare piece of Shinjuku that has somehow evaded the city's rapid, modern developments. Its name even sounds romantic – omoide translates to 'memory', harkening back to a simpler era. But before it was Omoide-yokochō, it was Lucky Street, a postwar-era black market of shops that stood back-to-back, separated only by wooden shutters. Even the ubiquity of *yakitori* (skewered meat) and *motsuyaki* (grilled offal) shops here can be traced back to this era, when offal wasn't rationed and could therefore be consumed in greater quantities.

clubs and bars don't take a cover charge.

When heading out, make sure to bring enough cash with you for the evening as not all ATMs run for 24 hours. But if you're in a pinch, look for Seven Eleven ATMs. Being able to speak a little Japanese can go a long way, even if it's just *arigatō gozaimasu* (thank you) and *onegaishimasu* (please).

Shop Fashion, Lifestyle & Latest Tech in Shinjuku

SHOPPING

To say that you could spend an entire week shopping in Shinjuku and still find more is an understatement. Shinjuku is home base to several large department stores: Isetan, Odakyu, Keio, Marui and Takashimaya – and that's not even counting the shopping malls and other stores in the area. The most fashionable (and high-end) department store is **Isetan** (MAP: 10 P118 **E6**; *mistore.jp/store/shinjuku .html*). **Takashimaya Times Square** (MAP: 11 P118 **D7**; *takashimaya .co.jp/shinjuku/timessquare*) carries luxury brands too and has lots of dining options.

Fashionable youths will want to try on the latest threads from local brands at shopping mall Lumine – there are three buildings: Lumine 1, Lumine 2 and **Lumine EST** (MAP: 12 P118 **D6**; *lumine.ne.jp/est*) and all are connected to Shinjuku

Station. The neighbourhood's newest mall, **NEWoMan** (MAP: 13 P118 **D7**; *newoman.jp*), carries sophisticated, high-end fashion brands.

Beyond fashion, **Books Kinokuniya Tokyo** (MAP: 14 P118 **D8**; *store. kinokuniya.co.jp/store/books-kinokuniya-tokyo*) is an excellent bookstore carrying English and other foreign-language books and lifestyle store **Hands** (MAP: 15 P118 **D7**; *shinjuku.hands.net*) has everything from stationery and toys to DIY tools and kitchen gadgets. Popular electronics store chain **Bic Camera** (MAP: 16 P118 **D6**; *tourist-info.bic-camera.com*) has its flagship store in the neighbourhood too, with all of the latest tech in store.

Go Thrift Shopping in Kōenji

SHOPPING

Kōenji's streetscape is a fascinating mix, encompassing record shops, fishmongers, barber shops, fruit stands, tattoo parlours, ramen stalls, pocket parks, artisan studios, micro-bars and live-music joints. It is also arguably Tokyo's top spot for vintage clothing stores. For a particularly populated stretch of shops offering great finds, head down the covered **Kōenji Pal Shopping Street** (MAP: 17 P118 **B3**; *koenji-pal.jp*) near the station's south exit and **Look Street** (MAP: 18 P118 **A3**; *koenjilook.com*), the open-air section lying beyond it. For local merch, art books, plushies, and even some weird and wacky items, have a look around at **Village Vanguard** (MAP: **19** P118 **A3**; *village-v. co.jp*).

Enjoy a Chill Evening in Nakano

Laid-back Nakano has excellent bars and bistros that make for a perfect quiet evening out with cocktails, wine and tapas. In summer, the restaurants around **Nakano Central Park** (MAP: **20** P118 **E2**) have tables and grills set up outdoors, and the park is a popular spot of families and groups of friends to have beers and barbecues. There are also lawns to spread picnic mats out and sip beers in the cool night air.

Tucked behind the shopping street on Nakano Station's north side is **Juke 80's** (MAP: **21** P118 **F2**; *juke80s.com*), an unpretentious bar where drinks are ¥500 and patrons can request their favourite English tunes from the '80s. If you prefer retro J-Pop and City Pop instead, head around the corner to its sister bar, **J-Juke 80's** (MAP: **22** P118 **F2**; *jjuke80s.com*).

Get Lost in Shinjuku Station

The world's busiest **station** (MAP: **23** P118 **D6**) is a behemoth. It serves an average of 3.5 million people per day across 11 train lines, so navigating through the sea of people and the station's system of corridors and underpasses is no easy feat – even for some locals. Recent station renovations have made it easier for commuters to find their way, but if you aren't strapped for time, wandering the station's hallways outside of rush hour can be a fun experience. Many of the buildings within Shinjuku are connected via underpasses from the station and you could quite literally walk from one end of Shinjuku to another without needing to surface. There's also an underground shopping arcade here called **Subnade** (MAP: **24** P118 **D5**; *subnade.co.jp*).

Best Places for...

¥ Budget　¥¥ Midrange　¥¥¥ Top End

See p118 for map of locations

Eating

Light Dishes

Lou ¥
25 F1

Portland-inspired Nakano cafe with a leafy terrace featuring coffee drinks, healthy salad bowls, scrumptious desserts, craft beers and natural wines. *instagram.com/ lou_nakano; 8am-4pm Thu-Tue*

Ochobohan ¥¥
26 D6

Ochazuke (rice eaten with broth) restaurant inside Lumine EST shopping mall. Bowls here are topped with fresh salmon, tuna and other seafood. *dd-holdings.jp/shops/ ochobohan/shinjuku; 11am-10pm*

Tsukiji Tamasushi ¥¥
27 D7

Comfortable midrange sushi restaurant inside Takashimaya Times Square. Set meals with assorted sushi are great value for money; à la carte orders available too. *tamasushi.co.jp; 11am-10pm*

Izakaya

Paikaji ¥¥
28 D7

Okinawa-themed *izakaya* opposite NEWoMan in Shinjuku. Laid-back tropical vibes and tasty Okinawan dishes, like *gōyā champurū* (stir-fried bitter gourd). *paikaji.jp/ shop/shinjuku; 11.30am-3pm & 5pm-5am Mon-Fri, from 4pm Sat & Sun*

Meat Restaurants

Gyūkatsu Aona ¥¥
29 D5

Tender slices of beef, breaded and deep-fried. The store is decorated with *nebuta* – colourful festival floats and lanterns from Aomori Prefecture. Near Kabukichō. *gyukatsu-aona.com; 11am-11.30pm*

MoMo Paradise ¥¥¥
30 D6

Popular sukiyaki hotpot chain with all-you-can-eat beef and a free-flow dessert bar. This branch is near Shinjuku Station's east exit; there's another just north Kabukichō. Reservations recommended. *mo-mo-para dise.com; 11.30am-3pm & 5-10.30pm; Kabukichō store open for lunch only on weekends*

Drinking

Hip Cafes

Hanbey ¥¥¥
31 D5

Retro 1950s- to 1970s-themed *izakaya* where old movie posters cover the walls and vintage music is piped through the speakers. The extensive menu even includes crickets. In Kabukichō. *hakuritabai-hanbey.com/en; 5pm-midnight*

Blue Bottle Coffee Shinjuku Cafe
32 D7

Shinjuku's premier coffee stand. Always busy; you can get coffee to-go and drink it at the terrace.

store.bluebottlecoffee. jp; 8am-9pm Tue-Sat, to 8.30pm Sun

Coffee Zingaro

 **F2**

This retro *kissaten*-inspired cafe inside Nakano Broadway is the brainchild of designer Takashi Murakami. The decor features his signature colourful flower motifs and tables double as gaming consoles. *instagram.com/cafe _zingaro; noon-7pm Thu-Mon, to 8pm Sat & Sun*

Golden Gai Bars

Death Match in Hell

34 **E5**

Take a trip to the underworld at this classic horror- and death-metal-themed bar in Golden Gai. All drinks aptly priced at ¥666. *instagram .com/deathmatchinhell; 8pm-3am Mon-Sat*

Bar Kinema Club

35 **E5**

This laid-back cinema-themed bar in Golden Gai has plenty of vintage film posters and autographs to admire while you drink. *bar-cinema.com; 6pm-late*

Open Book

36 **E5**

The grandson of award-winning author Komimasa Tanaka runs this sleek, modern Golden Gai bar that's lined up to the ceiling with shelves of books. *openbook.tokyo; 8pm-midnight*

Memorable Bars

Cocktail Shobō

 **A2**

Calm and rustic literary cafe in Kōenji lined with bookshelves. The food and cocktails served here are all based on recipes from famous novels. *koenji-cocktail.info; noon-3pm & 6-11pm*

Bar BenFidditch

 **C6**

This dark, rustic bar is regarded as one of the world's best. Cocktail ingredients often come from the owner Hiroyasu Kayama's farm and drinks are made to your liking. Reservations recommended. *facebook.com/ BarBenfiddich; 5pm-midnight Tue-Sun*

Shopping

Art & Collectibles

SUBstore

39 **A3**

Eclectic and friendly all-in-one bookstore, art gallery, cafe and event space that captures the laid-back vibe of Kōenji, loved by locals and visitors alike. *substore. jimdofree.com; 5-11pm Wed-Sun*

Shinjuku Kitamura Camera

 **C7**

Stylish multistorey camera store with a curated collection of new and secondhand cameras and accessories. Near Shinjuku Station's east exit. *kitamuracamera.jp; 10am-9pm*

Books, Crafts & Stationery

Sekaido

41 **E6**

An art and stationery supplies store spanning six floors with every pen, pigment and paintbrush imaginable. Near Shinjuku-gyoen. *sekaido. co.jp; 9.30am-pm*

Okadaya

 **D5**

Spread across two separate buildings, this craft store in Shinjuku has the area's largest selection of fabrics, yarn, buttons and much more. *okadaya.co .jp/okadaya_blog/store/ s100; 11am-8.30pm*

Ghibli Museum, Mitaka

Studio Ghibli (pronounced 'jiburi') has created some of the best-loved films in Japan (and the world), including recent Academy Award–winner *The Boy and the Heron* (2023). Master animator Hayao Miyazaki designed this museum *(adult/child ¥100/400)* himself and it's a wonderful reflection of the dreamy atmosphere that makes his animations so enchanting.

PLANNING TIP
Tickets must be reserved in advance, which can be done online. Sales open up on the 10th for the following month from 10am – and go very quickly!

Scan this QR code to purchase tickets in advance.

The Magical World of Ghibli

Studio Ghibli's films transport viewers to fairy-tale lands as well as ones not unlike our own, but where magic, unusual creatures and the supernatural intervene in unexpected ways. While Miyazaki is fascinated by machines – and many of his works feature steampunk-esque contraptions, he remains committed to hand-drawing – a rarity in contemporary animation and the artistry shows.

Even those unfamiliar with the works of Studio Ghibli, founded in 1985 by Miyazaki and the late Isao Takahata, will find this museum enchanting. Fans likely won't want to leave.

Exploring the Museum

Ghibli Museum, Mitaka, rewards curiosity and play: peer through a small window, for example and you'll see little soot sprites (from *Spirited Away;* 2001). A spiral staircase leads to a purposefully overgrown rooftop terrace with a 5m-tall statue of the Robot Soldier from *Castle in the Sky* (1986). A highlight for kids (sorry, grown-ups!) is a giant replica of the cat bus from the classic *My Neighbor Totoro* (1988) that under-12s can climb on.

There's also a small theatre where original animated shorts – which can only be seen here – are screened (you'll get a ticket for this when you enter).

COWARDLION/SHUTTERSTOCK

The film changes monthly to keep fans coming back. Special exhibitions, meanwhile, often feature storyboards, sketches or cel art from past or present Ghibli works.

Elsewhere there's an imagined workshop filled with the kinds of books and artworks that inspired Miyazaki, as well as vintage machines from animation's history. Naturally, the museum gift shop is excellent, with plenty of tempting character goods for both kids and grown-ups.

Detour Through the Park

The museum sits at the western edge of **Inokashira-kōen**, another of Tokyo's beloved green spaces, this one with woodsy strolling paths, a big central pond and an ancient shrine to Benzaiten (one of Japan's eight lucky gods). It takes about 30 minutes to walk through the park to the museum from Kichijōji Station (one stop before Mitaka on the JR Chūō-Sōbu line). Otherwise, Mitaka is the nearest station to the museum.

QUICK BREAK
The museum's **Straw Hat Cafe** has simple fare and is often crowded; other options can be found within Inokashira-kōen.

See p144
for eating,
drinking and
shopping
listings

Explore
Akihabara, Kōrakuen & Kagurazaka

Researched by Manami Okazaki

Akihabara (秋葉原) is where fans of Japanese manga and anime come to bask in the glory of their favourite media and buy exclusive merchandise from giant arcades, bookstores and merch shops. Kōrakuen (後楽園) is home to Tokyo Dome, an indoor stadium where Tokyoites flock to see concerts and baseball games. Near Tokyo Dome City is the serene Koishikawa Kōrakuen, one of Tokyo's oldest and most beautiful gardens. Near Kōrakuen, the cobbled streets, shrines and old-fashioned shops of Kagurazaka (神楽坂) offer a glimpse into the past. South of Tokyo Dome City is Jimbōchō (神保町), the world's largest book district with over 150 bookstores.

Getting Around

 ### Train
To get straight to the centre of Akihabara, follow the signs at the station for the Electric Town Exit. The JR and Tsukuba Express both stop at Akihabara. The Tokyo Dome area is accessible via three stations: Kōrakuen, Suidobashi and Iidabashi.

 ### Metro
Jimbōchō is easily accessible via the Hanzōmon, Toei Shinjuku and Toei Mita subway and the JR to Kanda. Kagurazaka is also directly next to Iidabashi Station. (East Exit for Japan Rail; Exit B3 for Tokyo Metro.)

 ### Walk
At weekends, much of Akihabara is blocked off to traffic. We suggest walking from Jimbōchō to Akihabara.

Koishikawa Kōrakuen (p138)
LO KIN-HEI/SHUTTERSTOCK

THE BEST

TRANQUIL GARDEN
Koishikawa Kōrakuen (p138)

ANIME & MANGA SUBCULTURE
Akihabara (p137)

AMUSEMENT PARK
Tokyo Dome City (p139)

NEIGHBOURHOOD VIBE
Kagurazaka (p142)

BOOKSTORES
Jimbōchō (p142)

Map Labels

Ueno

TAITŌ-KU

Kasuga-dōri

Chuo-dōri

Suehirochō

Shuto Expwy No 1

CHŪŌ-KU

Iwamotochō

IWAMOTO-CHŌ

Akihabara

Shin-nihombashi

Chūō-dōri

NIHOMBASHI-HONCHŌ

KAJI-CHŌ

Nihgin-dōri

Edo-dōri

Kyū Iwasaki-teien

Akihabara Gachapon Hall

HONGŌ

YUSHIMA

Hongō-dōri

Hongō-dōri

Kanda Myōjin

Akihabara

Akihabara Radio Center

SOTO-KANDA

Kanda

Awajichō

KANDA-TACHŌ

KANDA-NISHIKICHO

KANDA-SUDACHŌ

UCHI-KANDA

OTEMACHI

Uchibori-dōri

Shin-Ochanomizu

Ogawamachi

Komiyama Shoten

Meidai-dōri

Ochanomizu

Sotobori-dōri

HONGŌ

BUNKYŌ-KU

Gallery Soumei-do

Hara Shobo

Jimbōchō

Ogawa Tosho

Kitazawa Bookstore

Kokyo Higashi-Gyoen (Imperial Palace East Garden)

Kanda-gawa

Ōte Moat

Nihombashi-gawa

Kanda-Keisatsu-dōri

Kinbashi-dōri

Kiyomizu Moat

Ōte Moat

Hakusan-dōri

Tokyo Dome

Spa LaQua

Tokyo Dome City

Koishikawa Kōrakuen

KŌRAKU

Suidōbashi

MISAKI-CHŌ

Sendai-dōri

Shuto Expwy No 5

IIDABASHI

Iidabashi

Mejiro-dōri

Kudanshita

KUDAN-MINAMI

KUDANKITA

Kitanomaru-kōen

Area not open to public

SHINJUKU-KU

KOISHIKAWA

KAGURAZAKA

AKAGI-MOTOMACHI

Ōkubo-dōri

Ōkubo-dōri

Zenkoku-ji

WAKAMIYA-CHŌ

Ushigome-kagurazaka

Sotobori-dōri

Sotobori Moat

FUJIMI

Yasukuni-dōri

Yasukuni-dōri

ICHIGAYA-TAMACHI

Ichigaya

Edogawabashi

Akagi-jinja

Yarai Noh Theatre

Seekbase

500 m

0.25 miles

For more see

★	Top Experiences	p137
✿	Experiences	p142
✗	Eating	p144
🍶	Drinking	p145
🛍	Shopping	p145

Akihabara

Akihabara is almost a world of its own – one where 2D characters adorn billboards and soundtracks from the season's hottest anime is pumped through every one of the neighbourhood's speakers. This is the stomping ground of the *otaku* (geek), and whether you're a geek for anime or electronics, you'll find everything you want and more here.

MAP P136 **F2**

Otaku Central

The first place you'll want to go is Chūō-dōri. This is the main street lined with arcades, electronic stores, manga (comic book) shops, maid and cosplay cafes, and everything else an anime fan and otaku might be into. Grab a copy of the latest manga series and character merchandise at **Animate**, one of Akihabara's best-known manga stores; snag a coveted figurine at **Akihabara Radio Kaikan**; or just have a look around at all the capsule toys, plushies and other merchandise on display.

Akihabara's Roots

Before its streets were flooded with manga and merchandise, Akihabara was better known as Electric Town. In the post-war years, the neighbourhood emerged as the place to go for radio parts and other electronics, when radios were an essential part of daily life. The popularity of Akihabara as an electronics destination later paved the way for larger shops dealing in consumer appliances, when TVs and washing machines came along in the 1960s. To catch a glimpse of Akihabara's humble beginnings, head to the retro shopping complex **Akihabara Radio Center** (MAP P136 **F3**) near the station – it's a remnant of those postwar-era shops that today sell electronic parts, walkie-talkies and other vintage tech.

PLANNING TIP
To get straight to the centre of Akihabara where all the goods are, follow the signs at the station pointing to the Electric Town Exit.

Scan this QR code for an Akihabara Radio Kaikan shop list.

Koishikawa Kōrakuen

In the shadow of Tokyo Dome is one of Tokyo's oldest and most beautiful gardens, Koishikawa Kōrakuen *(adult/child ¥300/ free).* It's clear how much thought and effort has been put in to recreating some of Japan's most beautiful scenes in this miniature realm.

MAP P136 **C1**

PLANNING TIP
For the best seasonal blooms, time your visits for the months of February and June to see the garden's beautiful plum blossoms in winter and irises in summer.

Scan this QR code for more information.

The Edo Garden

First established as a garden for Lord Tokugawa Yorifusa's spare Edo residence, Koishikawa Kōrakuen was completed in 1629 and is the oldest among Edo's *daimyō* (feudal lord) gardens. The word Kōrakuen was derived from a Chinese phrase meaning something like 'worry first, enjoy later' – though that's not the only Chinese influence in the garden. The different scenes and landscapes you'll see can be attributed to Ming-dynasty scholar Zhu Zhiyu, who was involved in the garden's design by invitation of the *daimyō.*

Timeless Scenery

Much of the garden is based on other beautiful locations in Japan and China. The arched red bridge surrounded by maple is modelled after Tsūten-kyō at Kyoto's Tōkufu-ji temple, while the finest example of Chinese influence in the garden is the curved Engetsu-kyō bridge, shaped so that its reflection in the stream below resembles a full moon.

On your journey through the garden you'll pass through secluded wooded areas, trickling streams, rolling lawns, craggy rocks and colourful blooms. When you need a little break, have a seat on the benches overlooking the pond, designed to evoke Lake Biwa, a famous landmark northeast of Kyoto.

Tokyo Dome City

The biggest draw to Kōrakuen is the huge (by Tokyo's standards) sports and entertainment complex, Tokyo Dome City. At the centre is the baseball stadium Tokyo Dome, but there's also a theme park, mall and spa that make it one of the city's prime family destinations.

MAP P136 **C2**

Tokyo's Baseball Stadium

Completed in 1988, **Tokyo Dome** (MAP P136 **C1**) is an indoor baseball stadium that doubles as a concert and event venue holding up to 55,000 spectators. Home to the Yomiuri Giants, Tokyo Dome is the best place in the capital to catch a baseball game. It has also served as a venue for big international artists from Bruno Mars to Blackpink. Fans of Japanese baseball may want to stop by the **Baseball Hall of Fame & Museum**, also within the dome.

Thrills & Spills

In the vicinity of the baseball stadium are various theme park rides that make for an afternoon of family fun. The biggest (and loudest) attraction here is the rumbling **Thunder Dolphin** roller-coaster, which takes riders down a near 90-degree plunge before zipping through a hole in the nearby LaQua shopping centre.

Shopping & Relaxation

While not large, LaQua houses a good mix of midrange local brands and well-known retailers. If relaxation is what you're looking for, head upstairs to **Spa LaQua** (MAP P136 **C1**), which is equipped with natural hot spring baths and saunas, plus lots of space to relax and lounge in.

PLANNING TIP
Tokyo Dome and its nearby attractions fill at weekends and get quite crowded on event days. Weekdays are generally quiet.

Scan this QR code for more information on Tokyo Dome City.

Walk Akihabara

Akihabara caters to aficionados collecting according to their obsessions, rather than simply consuming trends. It's a sight every *otaku* (geek) recognises – neon arcades, colourful buildings topped with anime character billboards and maid cafes – this area just outside the 'Electric Town' JR train exit encapsulates the essence of Akihabara.

START	END	LENGTH
Seekbase building	Super Potato Retro-kan	1.5km; 2½hr

1 Retro Toys, Cameras & Vinyl

Start your tour of Akihabara (sometimes called 'Akiba') at the **Seekbase** building, preferably on a Sunday when Chūō-dōri is closed to vehicles. Browse the Godzilla and old-school anime toys at **Mandarake CoCoo**. Also visit the excellent vintage camera shop 2ndBase and vinyl store RECOfan on the same floor. Predicated on the fervour created when an item is 'limited edition', rare toys reach astronomical price tags as seen at Seekbase.

2 For Figure Fans

Still in the warren of shops nestled under the train tracks, towards Akihabara Station, **Tamashii Nations** makes high-quality anime and robot figures with meticulous builds; it also holds events.

3 Radio Kaikan

Next is the **Akihabara Radio Kaikan building**, a landmark of the neighbourhood. You'll find a dizzying array of trading cards, books, figurines, tech and audio equipment. The nine floors of retail are packed with merchandise; the 2nd-floor Astop is unusual in that it leases boxes to people selling off their collections. Each box is a peek into the collector's brain.

On the 4th and 6th floors, you'll see model car kits; some of the most popular are Japanese drift cars. On the 5th floor at Uchūsen Toys, there is a glass case filled with bears called Bearbrick; all have the same shape, but each one is a collaboration with a famous artist or brand.

4 Collect Them All

Love trading cards? Across Chūō-Dōri is the trading cards shop **Hareruya 2**, with six floors of Pokémon cards, with the world's largest inventory. There's an 88-seat play space with daily battle events at different playing levels.

5 Video Games Galore

Whether you're nostalgic for the games of your past or are just interested in the aesthetic, continue on to **Super Potato Retro-kan**, the retro gaming emporium with its great range of gaming consoles and games over three floors. In addition to systems such as Nintendo and Sega, you'll find old-school systems like the Game & Watch, Famicom and even Tamagotchis.

EXPERIENCES

Sift Through Old Tomes in Jimbōchō
BOOKS

Jimbōchō is known for secondhand books. It's a neighbourhood with a casual, down-to-earth vibe, as well as more than 150 bookstores with a collective inventory of some 10 million books. The shelves are stuffed entirely with old tomes in every genre and category available, housed mostly in old buildings. There's no telling what you might find here – every shop has its own eclectic selection, from novels, foreign languages and history to technical manuals. The excellent **Komiyama Shoten** (MAP: ❶ P136 **D3**, *book-komiyama.co.jp*) offers incredible selections of fine art and rare photography books. It also sells prints, posters and fashion titles, so even without knowing Japanese, there is a day's worth of treasures to trawl through. English books can be found in select shops like **Kitazawa Bookstore** (MAP: ❷ P136 **D3**, *kitazawa.co.jp*) and **Ogawa Tosho** (MAP: ❸ P136 **D3**). Most of these bookstores are along Yasukuni-dōri. The district is known for woodblock print stores such as **Hara Shobo** (MAP: ❹ P136 **D3**, *harashobo.com*) and **Gallery Soumei-do** (MAP: ❺ P136 **D3**, *soumei.biz*), which also sell contemporary prints.

Take a Look at Akihabara's Shrine
SHINTŌ SHRINE

MAP: ❻ P136 **E2**

A seven-minute walk from Akihabara Station's Electric Town Exit is **Kanda Myōjin** (*kandamyou jin.or.jp*). It was built in 730 CE near present-day Ōtemachi, and it is said that Tokugawa Ieyasu, founder of the Tokugawa shogunate, paid respects to the Shintō gods there. The shrine moved to its current location in 1616, and it's now a popular spot for visitors to Akihabara, who pray for love, luck and prosperity. Some of the *ema* – small votive plaques that are petitions for assistance from the shrine's resident deities – feature anime- and manga-style drawings made by visitors. The biennial Kanda festival, which takes place on odd-numbered years in mid-May, is one of Tokyo's three most famous festivals, with costumes and rowdy parades.

Explore Tokyo's Former Geisha Quarters
SHRINES, CAFES AND KIMONOS

On either side of the sloped street that runs through Kagurazaka's centre is a collection of quaint shops, cafes and cobbled lanes. Once a *hanamachi* – a pleasure quarter where geisha entertained – much of Kagurazaka retains an atmosphere reminiscent of centuries prior.

Stop at **Akagi-jinja** (MAP: ❼ P136 **A2**, *akagi-jinja.jp*), a modern shrine designed by famed architect Kengo Kuma in natural wood and glass. Walk east toward Iidabashi Station to pick up authentic souvenirs – thrift-shop for recycled kimonos, browse locally made tableware or pick up some freshly roasted tea at Rakuzan, a teashop that's just across the street from the 400-year-old temple **Zenkoku-ji** (MAP: 8 P136 **B2**, *kagurazaka-bishamonten.com*). In summer, the Awa-Odori Festival features a long line of dancers performing through the streets. In mid-October, the wonderfully quirky Kagurazaka Bakeneko Matsuri is a huge parade where everyone is dressed as supernatural cats. The **Yarai Noh Theatre** (MAP: 9 P136 **A2**, *yarai-nohgakudo.com*) offers both traditional and progressive *nō* performances.

Try for a Prize at the Arcades in Akihabara

GAMES & ENTERTAINMENT

MAP: 10 P136 **E2**

Arcades, or 'game centres' as they're called in Japan, are convenient places to stop by for a quick bout of fun. Brightly coloured, with plenty of crane-game cabinets stocked with famous characters that are immediately visible from the street, they stand ever ready to entice pedestrians into spending some spare ¥100 coins. They're found all around Tokyo, but Akihabara has a high concentration of them, including the big arcade chains GiGO and Taito Station. Don't miss the latest rhythm games, where the entire family can have fun playing the piano, *taiko*

drum and dancing machines such as Dance Dance Revolution, or simply watching the pros streaming their astonishing skills.

Also scattered around Akihabara and wider Tokyo are *gacha* machines (sometimes called *gachapon*), which dispense random capsule toys and trinkets for ¥200 to ¥500 apiece. The best *gacha* arcade is the **Akihabara Gachapon Hall** (*akibagacha.com*), although electronic shops such as Bic Camera and Yodobashi Camera also have them.

Shop Vinyl & Artisanal Goods

SHOPPING

MAP: 11 P136 **F2**

The row of shops under the train tracks near Akihabara Station's Electric Town Exit exudes an entirely different vibe from the rest of the neighbourhood. Instead of pop-culture and electronics, the outlets that stretch from here to Okachimachi Station are stocked with artisanal food, vintage vinyl records and handmade items.

Begin at **Seekbase** (*jrtk.jp/seekbase),* with boxes of vinyl records to sift through and vinyl figures of wacky *kaiju* (monsters) to gawk at. Further north is 2k540 Aki-Oka Artisan (p145) , a collection of 50 or so independent boutiques and ateliers selling handcrafted jewellery, fashion, accessories and interior items.

Best Places for...

¥ Budget   **¥¥** Midrange   **¥¥¥** Top End

See p136 for map of locations

Eating

Hearty Japanese Curries

Curry Bondy ¥
12 D3

Meaty, fruity, spicy curries and delicious puddings. A favourite literati haunt. *bondy.co.jp; 11am-9.30pm Mon-Fri, 10.30am-10pm Sat & Sun*

Topca ¥
13 E3

Come here if you like your curries spicy, with melt-in-your-mouth chunky meat and vegetables. *topca.co.jp; 11am-3.30pm & 5.30-10.30pm Mon-Fri, 11.30am-6pm Sat & Sun*

Gavial ¥
14 D3

More like stew than a curry, with large cubes of beef or pork and a mellow roux. *gavial1982.net; 11am-9pm Wed-Sun, to 4pm Mon*

Majicurry ¥
15 D3

The ultimate comfort food. Filling Japanese-style curry with breaded *tonkatsu* or hamburger patties on top. *majicurry. com; 11am-10pm*

Noodles

Tsujita ¥
16 E3

Slippery, slurp-worthy *tsukemen* (dipping noodles) served alongside a thick, delicious broth. *tsukemen-tsujita.com; 11am-9.30pm*

Mensho Tokyo ¥
17 C1

Chewy, freshly made noodles served in lamb knuckle and pork bone broth. Near Tokyo Dome. *menya-shono.com/tokyo; 11am-11pm Wed-Sun*

Tokyo Style Noodle Hotate Biyori ¥
18 F3

Clear and light *tsukemen* broth made from Hokkaidō scallops. *x.com/ hotatebiyori; hours vary*

Menya Musashi Bujin ¥
19 F3

Incredibly hearty *tsukemen* loved by locals. Its most popular item has a chunk of pork in it. *menya634.co.jp; 11am-10.30pm*

Tonkatsu

Marugo ¥¥
20 E3

Expect queues at this famed Akihabara *tonkatsu* (deep-fried pork cutlets) institution, but it's worth the wait: every bite is a crispy, fatty delight. *11.30am-3pm Wed-Sun*

Ippe Koppe by Tonkatsu Aoki ¥
21 E2

Local Akihabara *tonkatsu* spot: the *tonkatsu* is fried to perfection. Also try the *katsu* curry. *tonkatsu-aoki. com; 11am-8pm*

Tonkatsu Kenshin ¥¥
22 B2

Perfectly juicy, crispy *tonkatsu* with marbled fat at this popular Kagurazaka store. *tonkatsu-kenshin. com; 11.30am-2pm & 5-7pm Mon-Fri*

Agezuki 

23 B2

Savour the balance of pork, cabbage and rice in this Kagurazaka institution. As at all *tonkatsu* joints, solo travellers welcome. *ageduki.foodre. jp; 11.30am-2.30pm & 5.30-9pm Wed-Mon*

Cafes & Light Bites

Sabouru 

24 D3

This cafe's interior is reminiscent of a cosy log cabin and is full of rustic charm. Try the Napolitan spaghetti and colourful cream sodas. *x.com/ sabor2_jimbocho; 11am-7pm Mon-Sat*

Drinking

Book Cafes & Teahouses

Glitch Coffee & Roasters 

25 D3

A modern cafe serving serious coffee aficionados top-quality offerings. *glitchcoffee.com; 9am-7pm*

Final Fantasy Eorzea Cafe 

26 E3

A cafe that replicates the Final Fantasy role-playing game with cheap cafe food. *pasela.co .jp/paselabo_shop/ff _eorzea/; 10.45am-11pm*

Bumpōdō Gallery Cafe

27 D3

Cosy cafe and art gallery inside a stationery shop. Snag a sunny window seat for the best reading spot. *bumpodo.co.jp/ gallery/gallerycafe.html; 11am-6.30pm*

Jimbōchō Book Center

28 D3

Stylish cafe-bookstore popular for work and study. A comfy digital-nomad hangout with great puddings. *jimbocho-book. jp; 9am-7pm Mon-Fri, from 10am Sat & Sun*

Bars

Mogra

29 F2

Even if you aren't into clubbing, this anime soundtrack and J-pop nightclub has a great vibe (dancing, rather than sitting around drinking). *club-mogra.jp; hours vary*

Game Bar A-Button

30 F2

Retro game-themed bar in Akihabara, chock-full

of consoles, vintage collectibles and all things video game. It's tucked in an alley, but you'll know it immediately. *x.com/ a_button/; 5-11pm, from 4pm Sun*

Shopping

Books

Magnif

31 D3

Specialising in vintage fashion and lifestyle magazines, with more than 10,000 magazines ranging from subculture to fashion from the 1940s to 2000s. *magnif.jp; noon-6pm*

Ohya Shobo

32 D3

Rare books, Edo-period tomes, maps and *ukiyo-e* (woodblock prints). *ohya-shobo.com; 10am-6pm*

Souvenirs

2k540 Aki-Oka Artisan

33 F2

In this arcade, visit Nijyura for hand-dyed *tenugui*, the Japanese thin towels that are used for everything from kitchen cloths to sweatbands. Tokyo Noble has a dazzling array of umbrellas and parasols. *jrtk.jp/2k540; 11am-7pm Thu-Tue*

See p156
for eating,
drinking and
shopping
listings
アメ横
自転車専用
自転車を除く
一軒め酒場
売

Explore
Ueno & Yanesen

If you love art and museums, Ueno (上野) is the neighbourhood to visit. The majority of the sights here are within the massive Ueno-kōen (Ueno Park), including several temples and shrines, a zoo, the country's largest museum and a handful of other major institutions. Not far away, you'll also find the bustling street market, Ameya-yokochō.

Northwest of Ueno is a distinctly quieter and less populated area nicknamed Yanesen (谷根千), short for the three neighbourhoods of Yanaka, Nezu and Sendagi. Here you'll find cafes and art galleries in humble old buildings that have miraculously survived earthquakes, wars and the city's rapid modernisation efforts.

Getting Around

 **Train**

The JR Yamanote line stops at Ueno and Nippori (for Yanesen). Keisei trains from Narita Airport also stop at Ueno Station.

 **Metro**

The Ginza and Hibiya lines stop at Ueno Station. The Chiyoda line stops at Nezu and Sendagi. Ueno-okachimachi Station is also nearby, served by the Toei Ōedo line.

 **Walk**

Yanaka is within a 15-minute walk from Ueno-kōen, as is Nezu-jinja.

THE BEST

MUSEUM Tokyo National Museum (p149)

STREET MARKET Ameya-yokochō (p151)

OLD TOKYO ATMOSPHERE Yanaka (p152)

SHINTŌ SHRINE Nezu-jinja (p154)

GREEN SPACE Ueno-kōen (p154)

Ameya-yokochō (p151)
LEE YIU TUNG/SHUTTERSTOCK

ARAKAWA-KU
400 m
0.2 miles
NISHI-NIPPORI
Nippori
Yanaka Ginza
Sendagi
SENDAGI
Sansaki-zaka
YANAKA
Yanaka-reien
Hebi-dōri
Yomise-dōri
Sakura-dōri
Ogubashi-dōri
Kototoi-dōri
Uguisudani
UENO-SAKURAGI
Nezu-jinja
NEZU
Heiseikan
Gallery of Hōryū-ji Treasures
Tokyo National Museum
National Museum of Nature & Science
National Museum of Western Art
Ueno
IKE-NO-HATA
Nezu
University of Tokyo
Ueno Tōshō-gū
Ueno-kōen
Kiyomizu Kannon-dō
UENO
Shinobazu-dōri
Suijodobutsu-ike
Dobutsuen-dōri
Bōto-ike
Benten-dō
Keisei Ueno
Chūō-dōri
Ueno
HONGŌ
Shinobazu-ike
Shitamachi Museum
Kyū Iwasaki-teien
Ueno-Naka-dōri
Chūō-dōri
HIGASHI-UENO
Ameya-yokochō
Okachimachi
Yushima
Nakamachi-dōri
Ueno-hirokōji
Ueno-okachimachi

For more see
Top Experiences   p149
Experiences   p154
Eating   p156
Drinking   p157
Shopping   p157

Tokyo National Museum

The oldest and largest museum in Japan, the Tokyo National Museum *(adult/child ¥1000/free)* is a crash course in Japanese art and history. The six buildings within the museum complex house collections ranging from prehistoric Japanese artefacts to swords, temple treasures and even pieces from across Asia and the Middle East.

MAP P148 **D3**

Honkan (Japanese Gallery)

The sloped-roofed building directly visible from the entrance is the museum's main gallery, called the Honkan. Step through its doors and make a beeline for the upper floor, where exhibits are arranged in chronological order – beginning with ancient art, then tracing the evolution of classic Japanese art through the centuries, ending with Edo-period *ukiyo-e* (woodblock prints).

Descend to the ground floor to see exhibits ordered by craft and theme, including sculptures, lacquerware, swords, and Ainu and Ryūkyū art. There's also a fun interactive gallery that children will love. Step out into the museum garden to see the five historic teahouses that have been relocated here from across the country. At certain times of the year, you can drop by **Tohaku Chakan** *(tohaku-chakan.jp),* the grandest tea room here, for tea, sweets and cultural experiences.

Before leaving the Honkan, stop by the excellent gift shop to browse the collection of art books and merchandise – some featuring the museum's mascot, a *haniwa* (earthenware figure) named Tōhaku-kun.

PLANNING TIP
Make the Honkan (Japanese Gallery) your first stop and budget at least an hour here. Last admission is 30 minutes before closing. The museum is closed on Mondays.

Scan this QR code for full opening times and prices.

LEON RAFAEL/SHUTTERSTOCK

QUICK BREAK
Food trucks can often be found parked near the museum's main entrance, along with drink-vending machines. The Honkan and Heiseikan also have vending machines.

Heiseikan (Japanese Archaeology Gallery)

Connected to the Honkan via an indoor walkway, the **Heiseikan** houses the Japanese Archaeology Gallery. Behind the glass cases, here are ancient tools and crafts, tombs and unique and stylised terracotta sculptures from the Kōfun period (300–538 CE) called *haniwa*. The upper floor hosts special exhibitions that require a separate ticket for entry.

Gallery of Hōryū-ji Treasures

The **Gallery of Hōryū-ji Treasures** (MAP P148 **C3**) is quietly tucked to the side of the museum's main gate and is a real treasure trove. Inside the gallery's dark halls are intricate Buddhist sculptures that shine under well-placed spotlights. The room with gilt bronze Buddhist statues is easily the most beautiful display in the entire museum compound. All the objects here are from the 7th-century temple Hōryū-ji (of Nara Prefecture), and among them are over a dozen National Treasures and 200-plus Important Cultural Properties.

Finish your tour of the gallery at the Digital Gallery of Hōryū-ji Treasures, where limited-time interactive exhibits showcase reproductions of art and objects from the historic temple on 8K monitors.

Ameya-yokochō

Ameya-yokochō, sometimes called 'Ameyoko' for short, is one of Tokyo's largest remaining street markets, with over 400 shops crammed onto the street stretching between Ueno Station and Okachimachi Station. A walk along this lively thoroughfare takes you past bargain shops, streetside eateries, and a lot of snacks and treats.

MAP P148 **C6**

Ameyoko's Origins

Like some of Tokyo's *yokochō* – narrow side streets populated by bars and *izakaya* (Japanese pub-eateries) – Ameya-yokochō can trace its advent to the period after WWII, when it was a black market that sold food at a time when supplies were scarce. As for its name, there are two different hypotheses: some say it comes from the sweet stores that opened here when sugar was considered a luxury (*ameya* means 'sweet shops') while others think 'Ameyoko' may have been short for 'America-yokochō', as many of the black-market goods were supposedly obtained from American GIs stationed in Tokyo during the occupation years.

Bargain Hunting

The practice of bargaining has all but died out in Tokyo – except here. Ameya-yokochō is known for its bargain shops and low prices, and it's the best place to hunt for discount sportswear, satin bomber jackets and more snacks than you can carry. If that's not enough, some stores may still accept bargaining if you purchase a substantial enough amount. That said, it's a good idea to walk the entire length of the *yokochō* before deciding what and where to buy.

PLANNING TIP
Go in the afternoon and stay for an early dinner to see the street at its liveliest. Some shops close on the second or third Wednesday of the month.

Scan this QR code for a Japanese-language map and directory of Ameyoko's stores.

Walk Yanaka

Sleepy Yanaka is the kind of neighbourhood rarely seen in modern-day Tokyo, possessing an unassuming, old-world charm. Largely undamaged by natural disasters and WWII bombings, the wooden buildings, humble temples and understated shophouses here show a snapshot of Tokyo before rapid development. This tour can be tacked onto a visit to the Tokyo National Museum.

START	END	LENGTH
SCAI the Bathhouse	Yanaka Ginza	3km; 3hr

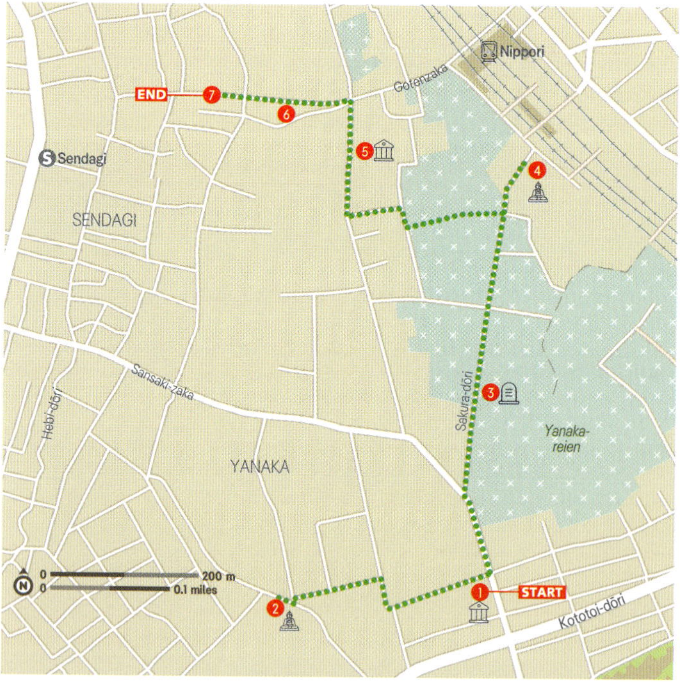

1 Gallery in a Bathhouse

SCAI the Bathhouse is 700m northwest along the road from the museum's main entrance. As its name suggests, this is a 200-year-old public bathhouse turned contemporary gallery. While the exhibition space inside is modern, the gallery has kept its traditional Japanese facade.

2 Runner's Temple

Turn left from the bathhouse and then a quick right, then left at the first junction. Up ahead, you'll see the **Yanaka Himalayan Cedar Tree**, a local landmark believed to be a few centuries old. A few paces from the tree is **Enju-ji**, a small temple enshrining the deity Nichika-sama, the God of Strong Legs. Unsurprisingly, the temple is popular with runners.

3 Quiet Stroll

Double back, then turn left at the bathhouse to get to **Yanaka-reien**, a quiet, peaceful cemetery serving as the final resting place for a few significant public figures in Japan, including the last shogun, Tokugawa Yoshinobu, whose grave lies beyond a gate marked by the clan symbol of three *aoi* leaves.

4 The Old Temple

Cut through to the other side of the cemetery and you'll come to **Tennō-ji**, a Buddhist temple that is one of the city's oldest, having been founded sometime between 1394 and 1427. Sitting serenely on the temple grounds framed by a modern entrance gate is a large bronze Buddha dating from 1690.

5 Bronze Works of Art

Exit the cemetery and make your way closer to town, stopping for a visit at the **Asakura Museum of Sculpture**. This was the former studio and residence of famed sculptor Fumio Asakura. Among his works you'll find bronze sculptures of famous Japanese figures, as well as cats, which Asakura was particularly fond of.

6 Sunset Steps

From the museum, go onto the main road, Gotenzaka. Then head west until you see **Yūyake Dandan**, the 'Sunset Steps'. The best time to see them is – of course – at sunset, when the streets below are cast in a romantic orange glow.

7 Nostalgic Shopping Street

The quaint and charming shopping street of **Yanaka Ginza** at the foot of the stairs is lined with produce and liquor shops, souvenir stores and some newer cafes. You might spot some cats here too – on the street and in the form of sculptures on the awnings. When you are done, Sendagi Station is near the bottom end of Yanaka Ginza.

EXPERIENCES

Walk under the Torii at Nezu-jinja
SHRINE

MAP: **1** P148 **A3**

Built in 1706, **Nezu-jinja** *(nedu jinja.or.jp; free; ¥200 for azalea garden in spring)* is among Tokyo's oldest Shintō shrines and the most beautiful. The major shrine buildings and gates are done up in gold and vermilion, including some iconic structures like the colourful, two-storey *rōmon* gate, which stands before the main shrine. Most of the structures have survived natural disasters and WWII destruction, remaining intact since their initial completion in the 18th century.

A second shrine, the **Otome Inari-jinja**, is located within the grounds. The path to this shrine is marked by dozens of small *torii* (shrine gates) you walk under to reach the shrine. Completing this picture-perfect spot are thousands of round azalea bushes that blanket the shrine grounds in white, yellow and magenta hues every year in April.

Go Museum-Hopping in Ueno-kōen
MUSEUMS

There are several museums within **Ueno-kōen** (MAP: **2** P148 **C4**; *ueno-bunka.jp*) besides the Tokyo National Museum that make for an afternoon of quiet wandering. Closest to the TNM, you could drop by the **National Museum of Nature & Science** (MAP: **3** P148 **D4**; *kahaku.go.jp, adult/child ¥630/ free*), where the permanent exhibition showcases dinosaur fossils, taxidermised animals and plants native to Japan.

After that, as you get nearer to Ueno Station, is the **National Museum of Western Art** (MAP: **4** P148 **D4**; *nmwa.go.jp; adult/ child ¥500/250*), which has an impressive collection of Western paintings from the 17th to the early 20th century, including pieces by Monet and Renoir. From there, stroll down to the southern end of the pond Shinobazu-ike, and you could finish with the **Shitamachi Museum** (MAP: **5** P148 **C5**; *taitogei bun.net, adult/child ¥300/100*). The

SAVE ON MUSEUM FEES

If you are planning on visiting a lot of museums and galleries during your time in Tokyo, pick up a Grutto Pass for ¥2500. This grants you access to 102 facilities around the capital, either for free or at a discounted price. Many of the city's art and history museums are included on this list, including all in Ueno-kōen. You can buy the pass at any of the participating facilities or online at *rekibun.or.jp/en/grutto*.

three small floors here give a vivid insight into Ueno's past, including reconstructions of homes and animated streetscapes.

See the Shrines & Temples of Ueno-kōen

SHRINES & TEMPLES

If you have time to see just a few temples and shrines, Ueno-kōen has some of the city's most prominent sites all within walking distance of each other. Start with the gold and gilded Shintō shrine **Ueno Tōshō-gū** (MAP: 6 P148 **C4**; *uenotoshogu.com; adult/child ¥500/200*). Built in 1627 in memory of Tokugawa Ieyasu, founder of the Tokugawa shogunate, the structure has survived earthquakes and wars and represents Edo-era architecture at its finest.

Afterwards, a short walk south will take you to **Kiyomizu Kannon-dō** (MAP: 7 P148 **C5**; *kiyomizu.kaneiji.jp; free*), one of Tokyo's oldest temples, built in the image of Kiyomizu-dera in Kyoto. The temple overlooks the lotus-covered Shinobazu-ike, at the centre of which is another Buddhist temple, **Benten-dō** (MAP: 8 P148 **C5**; *free*) – built with a circular, sloped roof to resemble Hōgon-ji, a temple on the island of the massive Lake Biwa in Shiga Prefecture. If you get peckish, the bridge leading from Ueno-kōen to Benten-dō is usually flanked by food stalls that lend a cheerful festival vibe.

Best Places for...

❥Budget   ❥❥Midrange   ❥❥❥Top End

See p148 for map of locations

Eating

Quaint Spots

Amane Saryō ❥
9 A2

A beautiful, cosy Japanese-style teahouse occupying a renovated old residence in Sendagi. Cakes are served alongside tea, and *teishoku* (set meals) are available for lunch. *amanesaryo.com; 11am-6pm Thu-Mon*

Onigiri Cafe Risaku ❥
10 A2

The *onigiri* (rice balls) here come with all kinds of toppings, paired with healthy side dishes and miso soup. Near Sendagi Station. *risaku-tokyo.com; 9am-8pm Thu-Tue*

Sweets & Desserts

Nezu-no-Taiyaki ❥
11 A3

A street stall selling *taiyaki* – bean-filled pastries shaped like *tai* (sea bream). They are very popular, so come early in case they sell out. *10am-2pm Mon-Sat*

Usagi-ya ❥
12 C6

A well-known, century-old sweetshop in Ueno selling *dorayaki* (pancake-like pastries filled with bean paste) and cute bunny-shaped *usagi-manjū* (sweet dumpling pastries). *ueno-usagiya.jp; 9am-6pm Thu-Tue*

Himitsu-dō ❥❥
13 B1

Kakigōri (shaved ice) is typically a summer dessert, but the ones served here are so popular they're available year-round. Queues get long. *himitsudo.com; hours vary*

Meat & Noodles

Nagaoka-ya ❥❥
14 C6

Izakaya in Ueno serving Spanish fare and juicy lamb chops barbecued in the restaurant dining space. A nice selection of craft beer too. Reservations recommended. *nagaoka-ya.com; 5-11pm*

Mon-Fri, from 4pm Sat & Sun

Isen Honten ❥❥
15 C6

This restaurant in Ueno invented *katsu-sando* – sauce-covered pork-cutlet sandwiches. *Tonkatsu* (fried pork cutlet) set meals too. *isen-honten.gorp.jp; 11.30am-3pm & 4.30-8.10pm Thu-Tue*

Kamachiku ❥
16 B3

This udon shop specialising in *kama-age udon* (noodles served straight in the cooking pot) is housed in a restored brick warehouse in Nezu dating from 1910. Sake pairings available. *kamachiku.com; 11.30am-2pm & 5.30-8pm Tue-Sat*

Ueno Menya Musashi Bukotsu Soden ❥
17 D5

Thick *tsukemen* (dipping noodles) topped with generous servings of pork that's perfect after a long day. Also serves ramen. *menya634.co.jp/storelist/ueno; 11.15am-10.15pm*

Drinking

Coffee Stands & Cafes

Kayaba Coffee
 C3

A *kissaten* (Japanese-style coffee shop) set in a historical wooden house in Yanaka whose interior incorporates sleek modern design. *instagram.com/kayabacoffee; 8am-6pm Tue-Sat*

Café Lapin
19 C6

Charming old-school *kissaten* in Ueno that roasts and sells its own beans and serves standard *kissaten* fare of sandwiches and cakes. *7am-5pm Mon-Sat*

Hagi Café
20 B1

Part of a complex in Yanaka that includes a gallery and hotel, this cafe is a good spot for a healthy Japanese breakfast. *hagiso.com/hagiso; hours vary*

Yanaka Komichi
21 B1

An ice-cream and coffee kiosk tucked down one of Yanaka Ginza's side alleys. *instagram.com/yanaka_komichi;*

11am-6pm Mon-Fri, from 10am Sat-Sun

Cocktails, Whisky & Craft Brews

Bar Bookshelff
22 D5

A bar for book lovers, by book lovers. Discuss your favourite books while sipping from the bar's extensive whisky selection. *barbookshelff.com; 6pm-1am Tue-Fri, from 3pm Sat & Sun*

Bousingot
23 A2

A funky cafe-bar in Sendagi where you can chill with a cocktail or a latte. Doubles as a used bookstore. *bousingot.com; 6-10pm Wed-Mon*

Cocktail Works Ueno
24 D5

Beautiful bar built to look like an urban kitchen, with inventive craft cocktails incorporating Japanese flavours such as shiso. *instagram.com/cocktailworks_ueno; 6pm-3am Mon-Sat, 5-11pm Sun*

Yanaka Beer Hall
25 C2

Located in a charming old building not far from SCAI the Bathhouse. Serves a range of its own brews on tap, including a refreshing wheat beer

and heavier IPA. Also has bar bites. *instagram.com/yanakabeerhall; 11am-8pm Tue-Sun*

Shopping

Charming Neighbourhood Shops

Yanaka Senbei Shinsei-dō
26 B1

Different varieties of *sembei* (rice crackers) line the display case of this neighbourhood shop, established in 1912. Perfect cheap and savoury afternoon snack. *10am-5.30pm Wed-Mon*

Nakano-ya
27 B1

A century-old shop in Yanaka selling assorted *tsukudani* (seafood and seaweed simmered in soy sauce and mirin). *nakanoya1923.com; 10am-5.30pm Thu-Tue*

Midori-ya
28 B1

Founded in 1908, this bamboo craft shop in Yanaka is currently under third-generation ownership. Peruse handcrafted chopsticks, interior items and more. *busekisuikou.com; 11am-6pm Tue-Sun*

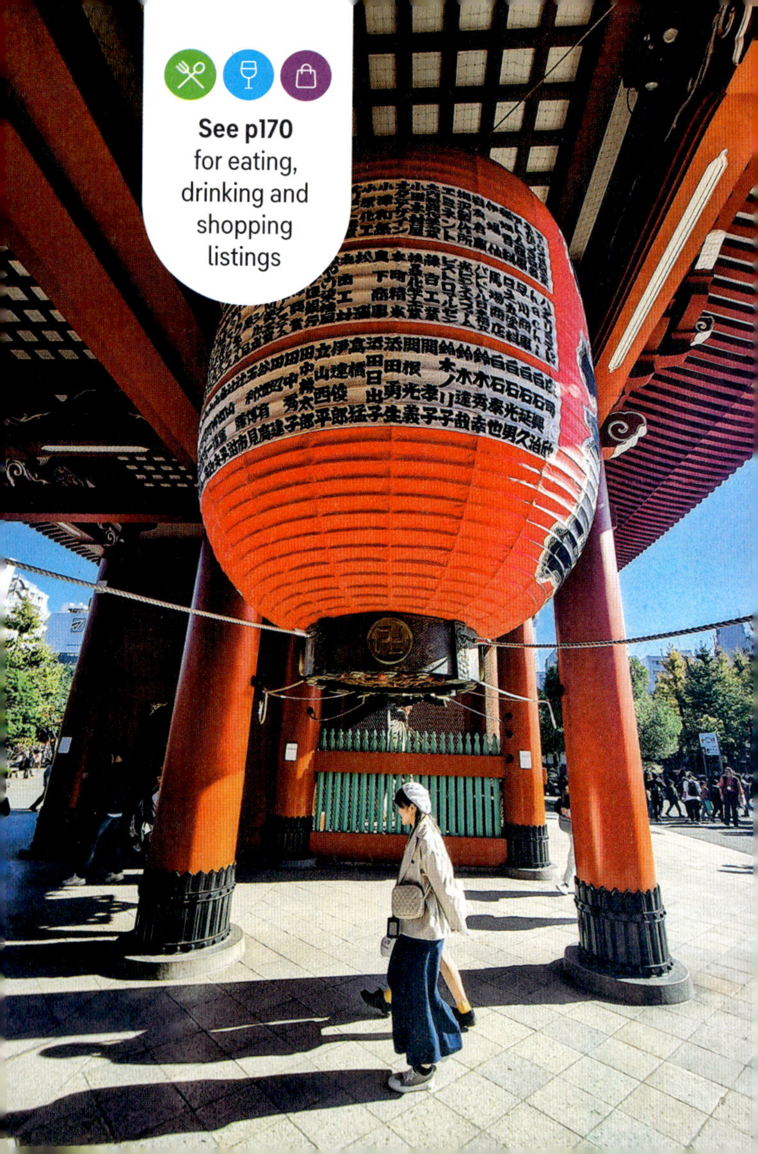
See p170
for eating,
drinking and
shopping
listings

Explore
Asakusa & Sumida River

Researched by
Manami Okazaki

Let the scent of incense waft over you as you step up to Tokyo's most ancient temple, Sensō-ji, while strolling the historical streets of Asakusa (浅草) in a kimono. Within walking distance of the temple is Kappabashi, where chefs and home cooks alike go to find cooking equipment and tableware.

Move south along Sumida River (隅田川) and you'll arrive at Kuramae, a neighbourhood of both traditional and modern artisans who work from small studios and run shops stocked with handmade items. Further south is Ryōgoku, where tournaments for Japan's national sport – sumo – take place, as well as the Edo Tokyo Museum, which takes you through the history of Tokyo.

Getting Around

 **Train**
For Asakusa use the metro Ginza line, the Asakusa line or the Tsukuba line. The JR Chūō line serves the Sumida region, and the Toei Ōedo line stops at Kuramae Station.

 **Walk**
The most convenient way to get around is by walking. Meander around the backstreets and small alleyways lined with local eateries and shops, and peek into residential life.

Rickshaw
While being pulled along on a carriage on wheels might not be immediately appealing, the experience of riding a rickshaw offers an filmic way to experience the district.

★

THE BEST

BUDDHIST TEMPLE
Sensō-ji (p162)

SUMO WRESTLING
Ryōgoku Kokugikan (p168)

UNIQUE SHOPPING
Kuramae (p168)

CITY VIEWS
Tokyo Skytree (p164)

NEIGHBOURHOOD STROLL
Kyōjima (p166)

Sensō-ji (p162)

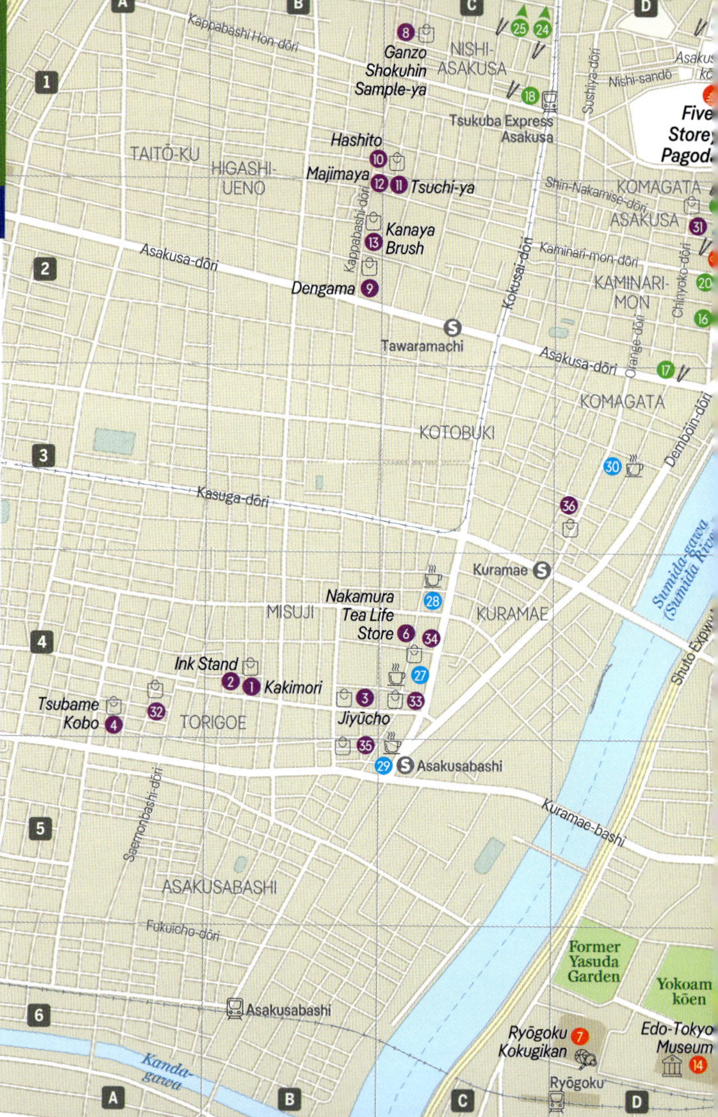

EXPLORE
ASAKUSA & SUMIDA RIVER
A
B
C
D
1
2
3
4
5
6
Kappabashi Hon-dōri
8
Ganzo Shokuhin Sample-ya
NISHI-ASAKUSA
25 24
18
Tsukuba Express Asakusa
Five Storey Pagoda
Hashito
10
Majimaya
12 11 Tsuchi-ya
TAITŌ-KU
HIGASHI-UENO
Shin-Nakamisé-dōri
KOMAGATA
ASAKUSA
31
Kanaya Brush
13
Kappabashi-dōri
Kokusai-dōri
Kaminari-mon-dōri
Asakusa-dōri
Dengama
9
KAMINARI-MON
Orange-dōri
20
16
Tawaramachi
Asakusa-dōri
17
KOMAGATA
KOTOBUKI
Dembōin-dōri
Kasuga-dōri
30
36
Sumida-gawa (Sumida River)
Kuramae
Nakamura Tea Life Store
28
MISUJI
6 34
KURAMAE
Ink Stand
2 1 Kakimori
27
Tsubame Kobo
4
32
3
33
TORIGOE
Jiyūcho
Saemonbashi-dōri
35
29 Asakusabashi
Shuto Expwy
ASAKUSABASHI
Kuramae-bashi
Fukuicho-dōri
Former Yasuda Garden
Yokoam kōen
Asakusabashi
Ryōgoku Kokugikan
7
Edo-Tokyo Museum
14
160
Kanda-gawa
Ryōgoku
A
B
C
D

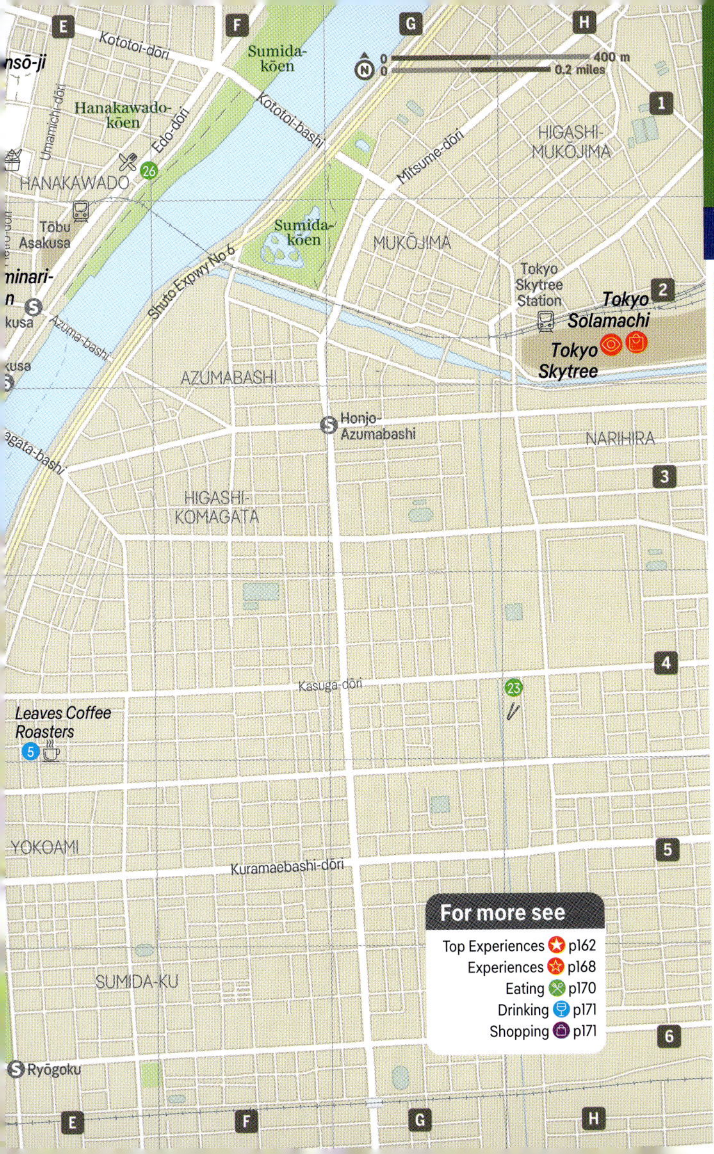

E Kototoi-dōri

F Sumida-kōen

G

H

nsō-ji

Hanakawado-kōen

Umamichi-dōri

Edo-dōri

Kototoi-bashi

Mitsume-dōri

HIGASHI-MUKŌJIMA

1

HANAKAWADO

Tōbu Asakusa

Sumida-kōen

MUKŌJIMA

minari-n

Azuma-bashi

Shuto Expwy No 6

Tokyo Skytree Station

Tokyo Solamachi

2

kusa

Tokyo Skytree

kusa

AZUMABASHI

Honjo-Azumabashi

NARIHIRA

3

agata-bashi

HIGASHI-KOMAGATA

Kasuga-dōri

23

4

Leaves Coffee Roasters

5

YOKOAMI

Kuramaebashi-dōri

5

SUMIDA-KU

For more see

Top Experiences p162
Experiences p168
Eating p170
Drinking p171
Shopping p171

6

Ryōgoku

E

F

G

H

Sensō-ji

The city's oldest temple, Sensō-ji, is to Tokyo as the Colosseum is to Rome – you simply have to see it. First constructed in the 7th century, this Buddhist temple enshrines Kannon, the Goddess of Mercy (hence why it's also known as Asakusa Kannon-dō).

MAP P160 **E1**

PLANNING TIP
This is a heavily touristed area and weaving your way through the crowd is part of the experience. Come back in the evening to see the temple lit up.

Scan this QR code for more about Sensō-ji.

Step Through the Gates

Kaminari-mon (MAP P160 **D2**), the temple's gateway, is the first thing you'll see approaching Sensō-ji. At its centre hangs a gigantic red *chōchin* (paper lantern). Step up to it to see an intricately carved dragon on its underside. Flanking the doorway are statues of two protector deities: Fūjin, the God of Wind; and Raijin, the God of Thunder. Originally built in 942 CE, it has been rebuilt several times – the current gate dates to 1960.

The Main Hall

Breathe in incense as you approach Kannon-dō, the main hall, then climb the steps and enter the worship area. To make an offering, drop a coin into the wooden box, put your hands together, and bow once. Kannon-dō was originally built by the third shogun (former military ruler), Tokugawa Iemitsu, and was a designated National Treasure before it was destroyed during WWII air raids – the structure that stands today was rebuilt in 1958.

Outside the temple's main hall is a **five-storey pagoda** (MAP P160 **D1**); originally built in 942 CE and also destroyed in WWII, the one that stands here now is a recreation. One of the city's finest pagodas during the Edo period, it was an important

ASAKUSA & SUMIDA RIVER   EXPLORE

JUJUMIN CHU/SHUTTERSTOCK

landmark of Asakusa and appeared often in art at the time. The top storey of the tower houses a Śarīra – a relic of the Buddha.

Seek Your Fortune

On New Year's Day, drawing an *omikuji* – a written fortune – from a temple or shrine is a Japanese custom, though you can do it any time of year. Just outside Kannon-dō, you'll see silver canisters placed before shelves laden with tiny drawers. Drop ¥100 into the collection box, give the canister a shake and flip it so that a stick juts out of a hole at the bottom. Note the character written on the stick, insert it back into the canister, and find the drawer with the corresponding character – your fortune lies within. If your fortune is good, you may keep it. Otherwise, tie the slip of paper to a nearby rack to ward off the misfortune.

QUICK BREAK
There's no shortage of food and snacks along Nakamise-dōri (p170). Ichiban-ya and Kimura-ya have been neighbourhood mainstays since the late 1800s.

Tokyo Skytree

At 634m, Tokyo Skytree *(350m/450m deck ¥2400/3500)* is the tallest tower in Japan and a majestic symbol of the city. It functions mainly as a telecommunications and broadcasting tower, but the observation decks offer sweeping views of the entire metropolis of Tokyo and beyond, and there's enough to do here to fill up a whole day.

MAP P160 **H2**

PLANNING TIP
Purchase a cheaper timed ticket online to skip the queue at the venue. Slightly discounted bundle deals for other nearby attractions are also available online.

Scan this QR code for tickets and information.

A Bird's-Eye View of Tokyo

Designed by famed architect Tadao Ando, needle-like Tokyo Skytree resembles something out of a sci-fi anime as the exterior latticed metal lights up at night in disco colours. It was completed in 2012 and altered the skyline of downtown Tokyo with its brilliant presence.

There are two observation decks: one at 350m and another at 450m. The view of Sumida River snaking across the metropolis you get from 450m above ground is worth the higher price. The best time to go is just before sunset – head up while it's light to see Tokyo in all its glory, then watch the city lights turn on as the sun creeps below the horizon.

Family-Friendly Fun

Pair your trip to the observation deck with a stop at **Tokyo Solamachi**, the mall and entertainment complex that's a popular destination for locals and tourists, particularly those with children, attached to Tokyo Skytree. Apart from shops (over 300 mostly midrange Japanese and international brands) and restaurants, the Sumida Aquarium, Postal Museum, a planetarium and a host of other

FOTOGRIN/SHUTTERSTOCK

attractions are also within the building, plus there's a sizeable play area on the 5th floor.

Pop-culture aficionados will want to stop by the Pokémon Centre and the adorable Kirby Café *(kirbycafe.jp)*. There's even more character merchandise elsewhere in the building – near the food court are stores dedicated to beloved characters such as Snoopy, Miffy and Rilakkuma. And if all that browsing and shopping is leaving you peckish, there's a wonderful selection of sweets and confectioneries on the 2nd floor. Dining options are also plentiful here; light bites are on the 1st floor, restaurants on the 6th. But for those special occasions, there's no better place to celebrate than the at restaurants with a view, halfway up Tokyo Skytree, on the 30th to 32nd floors.

TAKE A BREAK
There are outlets selling beverages, ice cream and snacks on both levels. Grab your refreshments and enjoy them with magnificent views.

165

Walk Sumida

Discover Kyōjima, a small community in Sumida ward that was largely spared from WWII bombings. Kyōjima is dense with tiny alleyways and cul-de-sacs, packed with street life both human and feline. Recently, many creators and artists have gone to great lengths to retrofit old buildings to save the town from development and fortify a sense of local community.

START	END	LENGTH
Art & Nepal	Denki-yu	1.5km; 1½hr

1 Sumida's Traditional Buildings

Start at **Art & Nepal**, a Nepali restaurant inside a traditional *kōminka* house that doubles as an art space called Kyōjima-eki. On either side of the street are examples of post-war *nagaya,* a type of vernacular wooden row house that once lodged artisans and labourers.

2 Converted Shops

Go down Kendama-yokochō to visit **Muumuu Coffee**. Owner Ayumu Haitani says that old properties for low rents and the freedom to renovate in this area made it easy to try out ideas. 'Through that, I've also met many people who share similar values. There are many in the community who value communication and mutual respect.'

3 Organic & Upcycled

Other spaces on the same street with DIY upgrades and real indie ethics include teashop **Satellite Kitchen**, serving a mishmash of tea, sweets and organic vegetables in a shabby-chic interior, and **wn penguin**, an upcycling shop with items like remade kimonos.

4 A Bustling Shopping Street

The road intersects with a traditional linear shopping street called Kira Kira Shotengai. These shopping streets are commonly found in downtown areas – usually with specialised food stores. Here there are numerous art studios and independent shops, such as **Kamos**, an indie bookstore, and further along to the northeast, **Nanzo**, a ceramics and art space inside a former futon bedding store.

5 Splendid Masks

Just past Nanzo is **Mask Shop Omote**, a shop selling both traditional and contemporary masks. The avant-garde store is run by mask artist and dancer Shuhei Okawara; some of the mask creations are simply incredible. Also, don't miss the traditional eateries still going strong that line the streets.

6 Hot Water

End your walk at **Denki-yu**, a spacious *sentō* (public bathhouse) that is known for appearing in the Wim Wenders film *Perfect Days* (2023). Denki-yu is the local *sentō* in Kyōjima that also host concerts and interesting exhibitions in the lobby and on the bathhouse walls. Soak in the restorative waters and sauna for just a few hundred yen.

EXPERIENCES

Buy Crafts & Drink Coffee at Kuramae
SHOPPING & COFFEE

Despite its proximity to Asakusa, Kuramae is quiet. It's home to many artisans and craftspeople, and several small factories and manufacturers are headquartered here, giving Kuramae a reputation of being a 'maker's town'.

Visit stationery store **Kakimori** (MAP: **1** P160 **B4**; *kakimori.com*) – there's a lovely illustrated map of the neighbourhood available for free here. Kakimori makes beautiful pens and custom notebooks that are very popular among locals. Right upstairs is **Ink Stand** (MAP: **2** P160 **B4**), where you can blend your own one-of-a-kind ink. On the way there, you'll also pass by **Jiyūcho** (MAP: **3** P160 **B4**; *jiyucho.tokyo*), a little letter shop where you can write a letter to your future self (reservation required). Also nearby is **Tsubame Kobo** (MAP: **4** P160 **A4**; *tsubamekobo.com/shop*) with hand-dyed and woven scarves.

For an afternoon pick-me-up, grab coffee at **Leaves Coffee Roasters** (MAP: **5** P160 **E4**) – the beans are fresh from their own roastery nearby. Tea drinkers can check out **Nakamura Tea Life Store** (MAP: **6** P160 **C4**) for organic green tea – direct from the owner's farm in Shizuoka – that comes in cool tin canisters.

Watch a Sumo Match in Ryōgoku
SUMO

MAP: **7** P160 **D6**

Standing by the banks of Sumida River, **Ryōgoku Kokugikan** is Japan's national sumo wrestling stadium. For 15 days in January, May and September each year, the giant fighters step onto the sacred *dohyō* (wrestling ring) here to fight, all in a bid to move up the ranks.

You'll know it's tournament season when you see colourful flags called *nobori* hoisted on bamboo sticks along the stadium's exterior – these have the fighters' names written on them, with the name of their sponsor underneath. Tickets for each tournament go on sale roughly one month before the day of the event on the Japan Sumo Association website *(sumo.or.jp; adult/child from ¥2500/500)*, with regular arena seating and box seats closer to the *dohyō* up for grabs. If you don't manage to snag a ticket before they're sold out, 400 general admission tickets go on sale at 8am at the stadium's box office on the day of the tournament.

Shop at Kappabashi
SHOPPING

Whether you're a professional in search of state-of-the-art tools or a home cook looking to purchase that special utensil that'll last a lifetime, Kappabashi-dōri is the place to go.

Along the 800m street and in the side alleys are approximately 160 stores stocking everything from knives, kitchen gadgets and lacquerware to pots and pans and – most interesting of all – plastic food samples. Inside these sample shops, you'll find the ultra-realistic bowls of noodles so often seen outside restaurants in Tokyo. Shops such as **Ganzo Shokuhin Sample-ya** (MAP: ⑧ P160 **C1**; *ganso-sample.com*) hold workshops (*¥3000*) for visitors to make one of these food samples in-store; sessions are in Japanese.

Shop ceramics at **Dengama** (MAP: ⑨ P160 **B2**; *dengama.jp*) and visit **Hashito** (MAP: ⑩ P160 **B1**; *hashi tou.co.jp*), which is like a museum of chopsticks with various wood types. **Tsuchi-ya** (MAP: ⑪ P160 **C1**; *tsuchi-ya.jp*) has a beautiful selection of glassware, including Edo-*kiriko* cut glass, made in Sumida. **Majimaya** (MAP: ⑫ P160 **B2**; *majimaya.com*) has a ginormous selection of baking goods, with hundreds of cookie moulds, and **Kanaya Brush** (MAP: ⑬ P160 **B2**; *kanaya-brush.com*) sells traditional brushes for calligraphy, beauty and cleaning.

Celebrate a Festival in Asakusa
FESTIVALS

If you find yourself in town during *matsuri* (festival) season, you're in for a treat. Many of these festivals are grand affairs that draw massive crowds; in Tokyo, few are bigger and more extravagant than those in Asakusa.

One of the major events early in the year is **Setsubun** at Sensō-ji, marking the beginning of spring in February. It's Japanese custom to throw beans on this day – a ritual

EDO-TOKYO MUSEUM
Next to Ryōgoku Kokugikan is arguably Tokyo's best history museum: the **Edo-Tokyo Museum** (*edo-tokyo-museum.or.jp*). Detailing the history of Tokyo from the Edo period to the modern day, the museum is an essential visit for anyone interested in getting a more in-depth understanding of the city and how it's been shaped over time. It has been closed for renovations for some time but is scheduled to reopen in 2026. In the meantime, you can see a life-sized recreation of Nihonbashi Bridge, plus the museum's many displays and dioramas, on the museum website.
MAP: ⑭ P160 **D6**

believed to ward away demons and bad luck; notable figures and even celebrities get involved, flinging beans off a raised platform to the crowds below. There's a special dance, with performers dressed as the Seven Gods of Good Fortune.

Another essential festival is the spirited **Sanja Matsuri**, a Shintō festival dedicated to Sensō-ji's founders. The May celebration sees volunteers carrying a *mikoshi* (portable shrine) through the streets. Over three days of bedlam, expect to see *taiko* performances, dancers, local geisha and participants with full-body tattoos in celebration mode.

Best Places for...

¥ Budget   ¥¥ Midrange   ¥¥¥ Top End

Eating

Edo-Style Food

Dote no Iseya ¥¥
15 C1

Housed in classic wooden building, serves saucy, hearty, Edomae tempura. *dotenoiseya.jp; 11am-2.30pm Thu-Mon*

Namiki Yabusoba ¥¥
16 D2

Founded in 1913 and serving delicious soba noodles with a strong soy dipping sauce; it is popular so expect to line up. *11am-7pm Fri-Tue*

Irokawa Unagi ¥¥
17 D3

Watch the chef cooking over the charcoal and savour the hearty, fluffy, smoky *unagi* (eel) at this eatery established in 1861. *gexc200.gorp.jp; 11.30am-2pm Mon-Sat*

Asakusa Midori Sushi ¥¥
18 C1

A sushi joint that locals love. Unpretentious with large toppings. *5-11pm Mon-Sun*

Nakamise Snacks

Funawa Nakamise Shop ¥
19 D2

A selection of sweet potato *wagashi* (Japanese sweets). Try the soft serve with its divine texture. *funawa.jp; 10am-6pm*

Tokiwadō Kaminari-okoshi ¥
20 D2

Puffed rice crackers going back to the Edo era in flavours such as green tea and almond. *tokiwado. tokyo/store/kaminarimon; 10am-6.30pm*

Kimuraya Ningyō-yaki ¥
21 E1

Sweet sponge cakes made in a metal mould in front of your eyes, filled with red bean. *10am-6.30pm*

Nakamise Kineya ¥
22 D2

Delicious salted rice crackers with an unique texture – it's difficult to stop eating them! *nakamise-kineya. com; 9.30am-6.30pm*

Vegan Eats

Sasaya Cafe ¥
23 H4

Spacious cafe in a converted warehouse with a terrace area; delicious vegan plates. *sasaya-cafe.com; 8.30am-6pm Mon-Sun*

Vegan Cafe PQ's ¥
24 D1

Spacious and cosy cafe that specialises in photo-genic, colourful curries. Also a queer-friendly space. *instagram.com/vegancurry; 11am-5pm Thu-Mon*

Bon ¥¥
25 D1

Well-presented, sophisticated vegan meals inspired by Buddhist cuisine. *fuchabon.co.jp; noon-3pm & 6-9pm Mon, Tue & Fri, noon-3pm & 5-8pm Sat & Sun*

Marugoto Vegan Dining Asakusa ¥
26 E1

Simple comfort vegan meals such as curries. *dining.marugotovegan. com; 11.30am-3pm & 6-9pm*

EXPLORE ASAKUSA & SUMIDA RIVER

Drinking

Coffee & Cafes

Dandelion Chocolate
 **27** C4

Enjoy a coffee or hot chocolate with a delectable selection of chocolate made in its factory. *dandelionchocolate.jp; 10am-7pm*

Coffee Wrights Kuramae
28 C4

Roastery and quaint upstairs cafe with a constantly changing selection of single-origin roasts. *coffee-wrights. jp; 11am-4pm Wed-Fri, 10am-5.30pm Sat & Sun*

marble Kuramae
29 C5

Stylish designer cafe with delicious cheesecakes. Has a quiet ambie/nce and is perfect for relaxing with a book. *instagram .com/marble_kuramae; 9am-7pm*

Hatcoffee
 **30** D3

Supremely cute 3D latte art specialists; they can also do dog portraits in your coffee if you show them a pet photo. *hatcoffee.jp; 10am-9pm Tue-Sun*

Shopping

Homeware

Seisuke Knife
31 D2

A large selection of glinting and colourful kitchen knives, on Shin-Nakamise-dōri shopping street near Sensō-ji. There are English-speaking staff. *seisuke knifekappabashi.com; 10.30am-6pm*

SyuRo
32 A4

Homeware store stocked with pieces by local artisans that are built to last. Products range from interior accents to personal-care items. *syuro.co.jp; noon-6pm, closed irregularly*

Proto Utsuwa to Takaramono
33 C4

A ceramics and decorative craft store with mini exhibitions featuring up-and-coming makers. *instagram.com/proto _kuramae; noon-7pm Tue-Sun*

Souvenirs

Maito Kuramae Store
34 C4

Every piece of clothing in this boutique is made from organic materials, and it's all hand-dyed in Japan using natural dyes derived from plants. *maitokomuro.com; 11.30am-6.30pm Tue-Sun*

hibi 10 Minutes Aroma
35 B5

Incense store that sells matches that give off exquisite scents, combining match-making from Harima with traditional incense from Awaji. *hibi-jp.com; noon-7pm Tue-Sun*

mt lab.
36 D3

A *washi* (Japanese paper) masking-tape emporium, featuring tape of every iteration that can be used for letter writing, home decoration, journals and art. *masking-tape.jp; noon-midnight, 1-7pm*

Tokyo Toolkit

Kabukichō (p122)

Family Travel

Navigating Tokyo's dense metropolitan landscape with kids can seem overwhelming. The general lack of space takes getting used to, but, luckily, safety is top-notch and many places in the city are equipped with nursing rooms and other facilities.

Eating Out

The go-to dining option for families with young children is family restaurants. They're reasonably priced and are equipped with spacious booths made to seat small groups, and typically have a large menu that includes global and Japanese dishes. Kids' menus are always available here. Popular chains in Tokyo include Royal Host, Denny's and Saizeriya.

Facilities

Malls and department stores typically have baby rooms equipped with changing tables and seats for resting. Multipurpose toilets with baby chairs and changing tables are also available at stations and some tourist attractions. Family restaurants and some larger restaurants will have highchairs available – ask for a 'baby chair'.

Nappies and other baby products are readily available at any chemist's, though brands and ingredients will be listed in Japanese.

TOKYO'S KIDS

Japanese schoolchildren are famously independent and navigate their way to and from school without adult supervision. It is quite normal to see young children crossing the street or riding the train by themselves.

Ticket Prices

Tickets to most attractions and public transport for children under 12 are typically half-price, and often free for those under five.

Breastfeeding

Breastfeeding in public is rare though nursing with a cover is generally acceptable.

Prams on Public Transport

If taking a pram onto the train, aim for the front or back of the carriages where there's more space. There are also carriages with more space for wheelchairs and prams – look for markings on the platform floor.

 # Accommodation

Accommodation in Tokyo runs the gamut, with plenty of options around the city that cater to every budget.

Where to Stay if You Love...

 ### Fashion, Nightlife & Style

Shibuya (p83) Easiest access to the city's trendiest shops plus lots of food options, and a lively drinking and clubbing scene. Very convenient, but also very crowded.

 ### High-End Shopping & Dining

Ginza & Tsukiji (p55) Tokyo's most upscale neighbourhood, Ginza, has luxury accommodation and cool boutique hotels. Hotel options in Tsukiji are more limited and less convenient.

 ### Museums & Culture

Ueno & Yanesen (p147) Ueno has a good range of options around the park and museums, and transport links are excellent. Yanesen has smaller inns, but is less convenient.

 ### Design & Architecture

Marunouchi & Nihombashi (p39) Lots of luxury hotels and modern ryokan (traditional Japanese inns) near some of the city's most interesting buildings and upscale shopping malls. Well-connected public transport via Tokyo Station.

 ### Lively Downtown Vibes

Asakusa & Sumida River (p159) This is a heavily touristed area with lots of hotels and hostels near major daytime attractions, lively bars and casual restaurants. Fewer convenient transport links.

OUR PICK

We Love to Stay In...

Shinjuku (p117) Most train lines run through Shinjuku Station, as do buses to/from the city's airports and other parts of the country. You also get to pick from a large range of hotels, from bare-bones capsule lodgings to luxury accommodation. This neighbourhood has endless things to do including shopping and all-night partying.

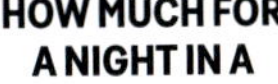

HOW MUCH FOR A NIGHT IN A

Capsule hotel per person
from ¥7000

Business hotel double room
from ¥12,000

Ryokan per person
from ¥12,000

 Food, Drink & Nightlife

 Allergies & Intolerances

If dining at a more upscale restaurant, you'll likely be asked if you have any allergies or intolerances when you order. Menus at chain restaurants may include notes on potential allergens, but not all dining establishments in the city will have this. Packaged food will always have allergens clearly marked, albeit in Japanese.

HOW TO SAY

I have an allergy *Arerugī ga arimasu*
Nuts *Nattsu*
Seafood *Shīfūdo*
Dairy products *Nyūseihin*

HOW TO ASK...

Is this gluten-free?
Kore wa guruten-furī desuka?
Does this contain nuts?
Kore niwa nattsu ga haitte-imasu-ka?
Can you please remove (ingredient)?
(Ingredient) nuki de, dekimasuka?

THE ALMIGHTY KONBINI

Tokyo's well-stocked convenience stores (*konbini* for short) are in a league of their own. With shelves lined with rice balls, tea, fried chicken, ramen and more, you'll be able to pull together a meal as healthy or as junky as you please. There are also ready-made meals that can be heated up in-store.

 Serving Sizes

Some dishes, like rice or ramen, often come in different serving sizes and you may be asked your preference when ordering. *Ōmori* means extra, and *nami-mori* denotes the typical serving size. Certain restaurants offer refills (usually of noodles or rice); to ask, say '*Okawari, onegaishimasu*' (Refill, please).

Pay the Bill

HOW TO...

It's common to pay before meals at fast-food restaurants, including those with vending machines, where you select and pay for your dish of choice. The machine then issues a meal ticket to be handed to restaurant staff. This is common at ramen restaurants and many popular budget diners like Yoshinoya. It's common for vending machines to take cash only.

At midrange restaurants, you may be brought a receipt or bill, called a *denpyō*, when your food is served. Take this to the cashier to pay on your way out of the restaurant.

If you don't get a *denpyō* (usually at higher-end restaurants), you pay at the table. Say '*O-kaikei onegaishimasu*' (The bill, please).

PRICE RANGES

The following price ranges refer to the average cost of a standard meal per person.

¥ less than ¥2000
¥¥ ¥2000–5000
¥¥¥ more than ¥5000

OPENING HOURS

Cafes 7am to 8pm
Restaurants 11am to 10pm, some may stay open later at weekends
Convenience stores 24 hours

Going Out

Bars and karaoke

The typical night out in Tokyo may involve beers and food at an *izakaya* (Japanese pub-eatery) followed by more drinks and karaoke once bars open up later in the evening. There's no shortage of *izakaya*, bars or karaoke boxes anywhere in the city, but Shinjuku and Shibuya are the most popular for all-night fun.

The club scene Most clubs are concentrated in the neighbourhoods of Shibuya and Roppongi. The latter has larger clubs and draws in more of an expat crowd, while younger partiers tend to prefer Shibuya.

When to go Bars start filling up after 9pm, and clubs after 11pm. If you're out past midnight, prepare to stay out all night until the trains resume, or shell out for a taxi.

Cover charges Many bars take a cover charge of between ¥500 and ¥1000. Clubs charge between ¥1000 and ¥4000 with a drink ticket included.

HOW MUCH FOR A

Ramen
¥1000

Gyū-don (beef bowl)
¥600

Sushi per person budget ¥2000 **midrange** ¥5000 **high-end** over ¥10,000

Nama-bīru (draught beer)
¥600

Coffee
¥500

Teishoku (set meal)
¥1000

Onigiri (rice ball)
¥150

# LGBTIQ+ Travellers

While discrimination is rare and high levels of safety can be expected, societal attitudes towards the LGBTIQ+ community tend to be reserved outside of neighbourhoods like Shinjuku Nichōme.

 ### Shinjuku Nichōme

Despite being one of the world's most densely populated cities, the only entertainment district specifically geared towards LGBTIQ+ folks is Shinjuku Nichōme, often referred to Nichōme for short. Though the area occupies a relatively small footprint, there's a high concentration of bars and clubs here, ranging from casual bars to themed clubs centred around certain interests or fetishes. If you don't know where to begin, hit a friendly bar like the **Aiiro Cafe** (p127), where locals and expats tend to start the evening – it has happy-hour prices and English-speaking staff. The atmosphere of Nichōme is warm and welcoming, and locals are always eager to meet travellers. However, some smaller bars may only accept regular customers or turn away non-Japanese-speaking clients.

Nichōme Highlights

(p127)

Bar Goldfinger Nichōme's most well-known lesbian bar. Open to all but it is women-only on Saturdays.

Dragon Men A fun bar near the entrance to Nichōme with a dance floor where pop hits are usually playing.

Arty Farty Small (and a little grungy) but popular club that gets very lively at weekends.

AiSOTOPE Lounge Dance club and event space with themed nights and sometimes performances.

TOKYO RAINBOW PRIDE

Japan's biggest Pride event takes place over three days at Yoyogi-kōen in June. Community members and allies celebrate the occasion with a parade, performances and more.

Need to Know

All-gender bathrooms are becoming increasingly available, but can still be sparse. If unavailable, all-purpose bathrooms may be used. Japanese society tends to avoid public displays of affection, regardless of gender or sexuality.

--- **PRIDEHOUSE TOKYO LEGACY** ---

A community centre offering resources and a safe space for all members of the LGBTIQ+ community. See their bilingual Instagram page for news and the latest events and meet-ups (*@pridehousetokyo*).

 Health & Safe Travel

Tokyo is exceedingly safe. Crime and theft are rare, though stay vigilant when it comes to to petty scams and natural disasters.

SUMMER HEAT

Every summer, heatstroke is a real threat to health and safety in Japan. Temperatures in Tokyo frequently reach above 35°C in July and August, coupled with very high humidity. If out and about, make sure to have a hat, parasol and sweat-wicking clothing, and hydrate frequently – tap water is safe to drink.

Earthquakes

Tokyo experiences periodic tremors, but large-magnitude earthquakes are rare. Most buildings in the city are reinforced against earthquakes and evacuation is rarely necessary. In the event of a major earthquake and other disasters, you should automatically receive alerts on your phone. Follow evacuation instructions – usually to a nearby park, school or community centre. If you are indoors, open the doors immediately, then hide under furniture. The multi-lingual Safety Tips app could also come in handy.

Touts

Ignore people touting cheap *izakaya* or clubs, particularly in areas like Shinjuku and Shibuya. Touting is illegal but common.

Typhoons

July to October is typhoon season, with most typhoons occurring around September. Expect strong winds and heavy rains that can disrupt business operations, and cause floods and delays to public transport – sometimes up to the next day. Heed warnings and stay indoors at your accommodation. Check the Japan Meteorological Agency *(jma.go.jp)* for updates.

HEALTHCARE

In the event of illness or emergency, call the 24-hour **Japan Visitor Hotline** on 050-3816-2787 for assistance in English. We also recommend purchasing travel insurance that covers medical care.

QUICK INFO

Privacy
Taking pictures of people in public is generally frowned upon. Your phone's shutter sound must be on.

Drugs
Possession of drugs, including marijuana, is illegal.

Public nuisance
Be respectful and avoid acts that may draw undue attention to yourself.

Responsible Travel

Follow these tips to leave a lighter footprint, support local businesses and have a positive impact on communities.

Low-Impact Travel

Tokyo's well-connected public transport system helps limit your carbon emissions and make quick, long-distance travel a breeze. However, much of the city can also be seen on foot or by bike, especially in central Tokyo. Stations are often within a 20-minute walk from each other or less, and you can discover a lot by choosing to walk. Bike shares are also available across the city via Docomo Bike Share.

OUR PICK

★

Upcycled Souvenirs

Check out upcycled fashion such as refashioned kimonos and quilted tote bags from independent shop **wn penguin** (p167) in Kyōjima.

Separating Your Rubbish

General waste is divided into two categories: burnable and non-burnable. Organic waste, napkins and soiled plastics are burnable, while clean plastic is non-burnable.

Good Ways to Hydrate

Vending machines are everywhere in the city, but Tokyo's tap water is also safe to drink. Pack a refillable bottle. If you prefer filtered water, get the MyMizu app to find refill spots. Lifestyle store Muji also has water refill stations at most of its outlets.

Resources

● **zenbird.media** News and stories focused on sustainable initiatives and social issues in Japan ● **sustainable.japantimes.com** Latest news on sustainability in Japan ● **japan meetings.org/why-japan/sustainability** From the Japan National Tourism Organisation

<hr>

SHOP FRESH & LOCAL

The UN University in Aoyama hosts a farmers market every weekend, where vendors from across the country bring in their own produce. Visit for a chance to sample the best seasonal offerings and get to know the people behind it all.

<hr>

Plastic Bags Be Gone

In 2020, Japan mandated that retailers must charge a fee (often around ¥3-10) for plastic bags, forcing consumers to opt in to using them, rather than being given bags automatically. In just a few years, plastic bag use plummeted by 80%. Plastic use per capita in Japan is still extremely high, but you can do your part by carrying an 'eco-bag' (local term for a reusable shopping bag) for your souvenir shopping.

VOLUNTEERING

Hands On Tokyo is a non-profit organisation maintaining a database of volunteering opportunities, from keeping elderly folks company to clean-up and food banking shifts.
See opportunities and sign up at *handsontokyo.org*.

Climate Change & Travel

It's impossible to ignore the impact we have when travelling; Lonely Planet urges all travellers to engage with their travel carbon footprint, which will mainly come from air travel. While there often isn't an alternative, travellers can look to mini-mise the number of flights they take and use cleaner ground transport, such as trains. One proposed solution – purchasing carbon offsets – unfortunately does not cancel out the impact of individual flights. While most destinations will depend on air travel for the foreseeable future, for now, pursuing ground-based travel where possible is the best course of action.

The **UN Carbon Offset Calculator** shows how flying impacts a household's emissions:

The **ICAO's carbon emissions calculator** allows visitors to analyse the CO2 generated by point-to-point journeys:

 Accessible Travel

 Public Transport

Wheelchair users can board city buses using an access ramp – the driver will get off and set this up, then arrange seats to accommodate the wheelchair. Some train carriages have designated spaces for wheelchair users and have a smaller gap on the platform for ease of access. Otherwise, station staff will assist you in getting on and off the train.

Taxis

Larger taxis that resemble London's black cabs can accommodate small wheelchairs. They're commonly found around central Tokyo, but if you need help hailing a ride, use the GO taxi app which allows riders to specify vehicle type based on accessibility needs.

MULTIPURPOSE TOILETS

Large, wheelchair-accessible multipurpose toilets are available at stations, department stores, museums and other public areas, and feature handrails, emergency-call buttons and sinks for ostomy-bag users.

Accommodation

Budget business and luxury hotels in Tokyo typically have one to several barrier-free rooms, but they may not be available at older hotels or ryokan.

STATIONS

Train stations are generally accessible and are equipped with tactile paving and elevators. Be sure to notify station staff before you board the train and they can arrange for staff to meet you at your destination.

Resources

● **accessible-japan.com** The most comprehensive guide to accessible travel in Japan, including reviews, hotel listings and tours.

Nuts & Bolts

Opening Hours

Bars, clubs and restaurants may have extended opening hours at weekends, and close early on Sundays. Some local businesses take Wednesdays off.

Cafes 7am–8pm

Bars 6pm–3am or later

Clubs 10pm–4am or later

Museums 10am–5pm

Restaurants 11am–2pm and 5–10pm

Shops 10am–8pm

Banks 9am–3pm Mon–Fri

Supermarkets 8am–9pm or later

Open
営業中
(Eigyōchū)

Closed
準備中
(Jyunbichū)

QUICK INFO

Time zone
GMT+9
Country calling code
+81
Emergency number
119
Population
14 million

ELECTRICITY
120V/60Hz

Smoking

Smoking (including vaping and electronic cigarettes) is prohibited except in designated smoking areas. Malls, some cafes and commercial buildings have smoking rooms.

Unless specified otherwise, bars and clubs usually allow smoking indoors. If you need an ashtray, say *'Haizara, onegaishimasu'*.

Public Holidays

Some businesses may be closed for an extended period during Obon (13–15 August) and year-end holidays.

New Year's Day 1 January

Coming of Age Day 2nd Monday in January

National Foundation Day 11 February

Emperor's Birthday 23 February

Shōwa Day 29 April

Constitution Day 3 May

Green Day 4 May

Children's Day 5 May

Marine Day 3rd Monday in July

Mountain Day 11 August

Respect for the Aged Day 3rd Monday in September

Sports Day 2nd Monday in October

Culture Day 3 November

Labour Thanksgiving Day 23 November

Language

Basics

Hello
こんにちは
kon·ni·chi·wa

Goodbye (Informal)
またね
mata·ne

Yes
はい *hai*

No
いいえ *ī·e*

Please
ください
ku·da·sai

Thank you
ありがとう
a·ri·ga·tō

Excuse me
すみません
su·mi·ma·sen

Sorry
ごめんなさい
go·men·na·sai

Cheers!
乾杯!
kan·pai

Fast Phrases

How are you?
お元気ですか?
o·gen·ki desu ka

Fine. And you?
はい元気です。あなたは?
hai, gen·ki desu a·na·ta wa

Do you speak English?
英語が 話せますか?
ē·go ga ha·na·se·masu ka

I'd like to reserve a table for (two)
(2人)の予約をお願いします
(fu·ta·ri) no yo·ya·ku wo o·ne·gai shi·masu

I'd like (the menu)
(メニュー)をお願いします
(me·nyū) wo o·ne·gai shi·masu

I don't eat (red meat)
(赤身の肉)は食べません
(a·ka·mi no ni·ku)wa ta·be·ma·sen

That was delicious
おいしかった
oy·shi·kat·ta

Please bring the bill
お勘定をください
o·kan·jō wo ku·da·sai

Numbers

 一 *i·chi*

 二 *ni*

 三 *san*

 四 *shi/yon*

 五 *go*

GOOD TO KNOW

Japanese pronunciation is easy for English speakers, as most of its sounds are also found in English. Note though that it's important to make the distinction between short and long vowels, as vowel length can change the meaning of a word. The long vowels (ā, ē, ī, ō, ū) should be held twice as long as the short ones. All syllables in a word are pronounced fairly evenly in Japanese. If you read our pronunciation guides as if they were English, you'll be understood.

Time & Numbers

What time is it?

何時ですか? — *nan·ji desu ka*

It's (10) o'clock

（10）時です — *(jū)·ji desu*

morning	朝	*a·sa*
afternoon	午後	*go·go*
evening	夕方	*yū·ga·ta*
yesterday	きのう	*ki·nō*
today	今日	*kyō*
tomorrow	明日	*a·shi·ta*

Signs

Entrance	入口		**Danger**	危険
Exit	出口		**Toilets**	トイレ
Information			**Men**	男
インフォメーション			**Women**	女

EMERGENCIES

Help!
たすけて！ *tasu·ke·te*

Go away!
離れろ！ *ha·na·re·ro*

Call the police!
警察を呼んで！
kē·sa·tsu wo yon·de

Call a doctor!
医者を呼んで！
i·sha wo yon·de

I'm lost.
迷いました
ma·yo·i·mashita

I'm ill.
私は病気です
wa·ta·shi wa byō·ki desu

It hurts here.
ここが痛いです。
ko·ko ga i·tai des

Where are the toilets?
トイレはどこですか?
toi·re wa doko desu ka

Index

Sights p000   Map pages p000

Eating

 **Drinking**

1Oak Tokyo 81

 **A**

Adezakura 127
Aiiro Cafe 127
AiSOTOPE Lounge 127
Aoyama Flower Market's Green
    House 111
Aroma Coffee Yaesu 53
Arty Farty 127

B

Bar BenFidditch 131
Bar Bookshelff 157
Bar Butler 66
Bar Gari Gari 95
Bar Goldfinger 127
Bar Kinema Club 131
Bar Luther 81
Bar Martha 96
Bar Track 96
Bar Trench 93
Bear Pond Espresso 96
Blue Bottle Coffee Shinjuku
    Cafe 130
Blue Note Place 89
Bongen Coffee 53
Bousingot 157
Bridge Coffee & Ice Cream 53
Bumpōdō Gallery Cafe 145

 **C**

Cafe de l'Ambre 34
Café de l'Ambre 66
Café Lapin 35, 157
Cafe Paulista 34, 63
Cocktail Shobō 131
Cocktail Works Ueno 157
Coffee Wrights Kuramae 171
Coffee Zingaro 131

 **D**

Dandelion Chocolate 171
Death Match in Hell 131
Dragon Men 127

 **E**

Eagle Tokyo Blue 127

 **F**

Final Fantasy Eorzea Cafe 145

 **G**

Game Bar A-Button 145
Glitch Coffee & Roasters 145
Good Coffee Farms Cafe 53
G's Bar 81

 **H**

Hagi Café 157
Hanbey 130
Harlem 94
Hatcoffee 171
Heiwa Doburoku Kabutocho 52
Hitachino Brewing 52
Hoshino Coffee 85

 **I**

Ippuku & Matcha 52

 **J**

Janai Coffee 97
Jimbōchō 35
Jimbōchō Book Center 145
J-Juke 80's 129
Juke 80's 129

 **K**

Karaoke-kan 94
Kayaba Coffee 35, 157
kissaten 95

 **L**

Leaves Coffee Roasters 168
Lion 35, 95
Little Nap Coffee Stand 114
Little Smith 66
Log Road Daikanyama 97

 **M**

Magnet by 109 85
Mandarin Bar 52
marble Kuramae 171
Matsubaya Saryō 114
Mogra 145
Muumuu Coffee 167

 **N**

Nomu 112

 **O**

O-East 94
Open Book 131

P

PR Bar 114
Punch Room 66

 **R**

Record Bar Analog 94
Roastery by Nozy 114
Rooftop Bar at Andaz Tokyo 81

S

Sakurai Japanese Tea
    Experience 114
Sarutahiko Coffee The Bridge
    107
Satellite Kitchen 167
Shisha Bar Rakuen 81
Sound Bar Howl 94

 **T**

Tapirosu 81
These 81
Tír na nÓg 66
Tohaku Chakan 149
Tsuruya Yoshinobu Tokyo
    Mise 53
Turret Coffee 66
Two Rooms 114

 **V**

Virtù 52

 **W**

Wang De Chuan 52
Wasachi 81
Womb 94

Y

Yanaka Beer Hall 157
Yanaka Komichi 157
Yebisu Brewery Tokyo 88
Yonemoto Coffee 66

 **Shopping**

2k540 Aki-Oka Artisan 145
6% Doki Doki 115

 **A**

Akihabara Radio Center 137
Akihabara Radio Kaikan 137
Akihabara Radio Kaikan building
    141
Animate 137
Azabu-jūban Street 75, 77

 **B**

Beams Harajuku 115
Bic Camera 128

Send Us Your Feedback

We love to hear from travellers – your comments help make our books better. We read every word, and we guarantee that your feedback goes straight to the authors. Visit lonelyplanet.com/contact to submit your updates and suggestions.

Note: We may edit, reproduce and incorporate your comments in Lonely Planet products such as guidebooks, websites and digital products, so let us know if you are happy to have your name acknowledged. For a copy of our privacy policy visit lonelyplanet.com/legal.

Acknowledgements

Cover photograph: Neon signs, Akihabara. KenSoftTH/Shutterstock

Back photograph: Sensō-ji. Fuchslocher/Shutterstock

THIS BOOK

The 11th edition of Lonely Planet's Pocket Tokyo guidebook was researched and written by Selena Takigawa Hoy, Cherise Fong, Todd Fong, Rob Goss, Kim Kahan, Louise George Kittaka and Manami Okazaki. The previous edition was written by Rebecca Milner and Winnie Tan. This guidebook was produced by the following:

Destination Editor
Selena Hoy

Coordinating Editor
Bridget Blair

Cartographers
Hunor Csutoros, Rachel Imeson

Production Editor
Jennifer McCann

Image Editor
Rie Miyoshi

Assisting Editors
Peterjon Cresswell, Lucy Jones, Jenna Myers, Charlotte Orr

Cover Researcher
Sam Ubinas

Thanks to
Fergal Condon, Gwen Cotter, Alison Killilea, Kellie Langdon, Saralinda Turner, Darren O'Connell

Although the authors and Lonely Planet have taken all reasonable care in preparing this book, we make no warranty about the accuracy or completeness of its content and, to the maximum extent permitted, disclaim all liability arising from its use.

Published by Lonely Planet Global Limited

CRN 554153

11th edition – Jul 2026

ISBN 978 1 83869 923 9

© Lonely Planet 2026

10 9 8 7 6 5 4 3 2 1

Printed in Malaysia

Paper in this book is certified against the Forest Stewardship Council™ standards. FSC™ promotes environmentally responsible, socially beneficial and economically viable management of the world's forests.